Public Insurance
in Private
Medical Markets

Public Insurance in Private Medical Markets

Some Problems of National Health Insurance

H. E. Frech III
and
Paul B. Ginsburg

American Enterprise Institute for Public Policy Research
Washington, D.C.

H.E. Frech III is an associate professor of economics at the University of California at Santa Barbara.

Paul B. Ginsburg is an associate professor of policy sciences and of community health sciences at Duke University and director of Duke's Center for the Study of Health Policy.

Library of Congress Cataloging in Publication Data

Frech, H. E.
    Public insurance in private medical markets.

    (AEI studies ; 201)
    A revision and expansion of the authors' paper originally published in Economic inquiry, v. 13, no. 1 (March 1975)
    Includes bibliographical references.
    1. Insurance, Health—United States.
I. Ginsburg, Paul B., joint author. II. Title.
III. Series: American Enterprise Institute for Public Policy Research. AEI studies ; 201.
HD7102.U4F65   368.4'2'00973   78-18404
ISBN 0-8447-3303-2

Printed in the United States of America

CONTENTS

PREFACE

This study grew out of Robert B. Helms's encouragement to redo a paper we had published in an economics journal in a new, more policy-oriented form.[1] The original paper compared various methods of fee or price regulation in medical care and different mechanisms for consumer copayment. In recasting the paper for a new audience, we discovered that a comprehensive treatment of the policy issues involved in designing benefits under national health insurance required a broader approach. As a result, we added three major topics not addressed in the original paper: a discussion of the general problem of public insurance in private markets (chapter 2), an examination of the health maintenance organization as an innovation for dealing with problems inherent in third-party market relationships (chapter 5), and a discussion of policy alternatives (chapter 6). A discussion of the appropriateness of economic analysis for dealing with issues of medical care resource allocation (Appendix A) has also been included.

We wish to thank Bob Helms for the prodding necessary to get us started on this work, as well as for very important comments on an early draft. We are also grateful to Lee Benham and Yale Brozen for useful comments on an earlier version. Finally, we are indebted to the Johnson Foundation for its support of Frech in the form of a Johnson Foundation Faculty Fellowship in the department of economics, Harvard University, during the final stages of preparing the study.

[1] H. E. Frech III and Paul B. Ginsburg, "Imposed Health Insurance in Monopolistic Markets: A Theoretical Analysis," *Economic Inquiry*, vol. 13, no. 1 (March 1975), pp. 55–70.

1
Introduction

National health insurance (NHI) is a leading issue in the United States today. Put simply, the question is whether the federal government should expand its role in financing medical care. Currently, the federal government finances health care for the elderly (Medicare), makes grants to states which finance health care for the poor (Medicaid), and subsidizes hospital construction (Hill-Burton, FHA). Also, government-operated hospitals, outpatient facilities, and nursing homes provide care directly to military personnel, veterans, merchant seamen, American Indians, and a small number of the poor.

Proposals to expand this role include using the income tax system to provide insurance directly, subsidizing the purchase of private insurance, providing public insurance to all, and requiring employers to provide comprehensive insurance to employees. Forty-five separate NHI plans were introduced into the ninety-fifth Congress.[1] Virtually all the organized interest groups in the health care system have either had a bill introduced or testified in support of one.[2] While many of these groups, such as physicians and health insurers, probably do not support an expanded federal role in the medical care system, they have nevertheless developed proposals for limited changes in an attempt to head off more major changes.

A notable theme that runs through all the proposals, from conservative to liberal, is that government should not expand its direct provision function (although there is no pressure either to cut back

---

[1] U.S. Department of Health, Education, and Welfare, Social Security Administration, *National Health Insurance Proposals: Provisions of Bills Introduced in the 93rd Congress as of July 1974*, DHEW publication no. (SSA) 75–11920, 1974.

[2] See, for example, U.S. Congress, House, Committee on Ways and Means, Subcommittee on Health, *Hearings on National Health Insurance*, 94th Congress, 1st session, November-December 1975.

direct federal provision)[3]: all envision a continuation of privately provided medical care. This is clearly the case in the proposals for expanding the use of private insurance. But even those that envision public insurance see it in the context of private provision of care. While regulation of the private market would increase under some of the proposals, physicians will not be considered government employees, though of course regulation could make physicians de facto government employees.

A great deal has been written on the subject of NHI,[4] discussing such issues as who should be covered (the entire population or only the needy), the scope of benefits, whether cost sharing should be used, and whether the federal government or private companies should provide the insurance. One aspect given relatively little attention is what type of benefits the government (or private insurers acting for it) should provide for consumers in the private medical market. This interaction of public insurance and private health care markets is complex and deserving of more attention. It is the concern of this monograph.

Many have argued the importance of consumer out-of-pocket expenses in restraining the demand for health care, thus reducing costs. We expand the question to include the impact of copayments or their absence on the entire health care system. We find that consumer out-of-pocket expenses are absolutely necessary for a decentralized allocation of health care that is responsive to consumer wants. Further, even for a given dollar amount of consumer out-of-pocket payments, the exact type of copayment turns out to be important. The alternative would be some form of nonprice rationing. Nonprice rationing within competing private organizations (called health maintenance organizations or HMOs) can be very useful, but when done in a govern-

---

[3] Conservatives oppose public provision to minimize the role of government in the medical care system. Liberals also oppose it because of the risk of inferior standards of service for the disadvantaged. Cotton Lindsay has proposed a reduction of direct provision in *Veterans Administration Hospitals: An Economic Analysis of Government Enterprise* (Washington, D.C.: American Enterprise Institute, 1975), pp. 77–78.

[4] For example, Karen Davis, *National Health Insurance: Benefits, Costs, and Consequences* (Washington, D.C.: Brookings Institution, 1975); Walter McClure, "The Medical Care System under National Health Insurance: Four Models," *Journal of Health Politics, Policy and Law*, vol. 1, no. 1 (January 1976), pp. 22–111; Mark V. Pauly, *National Health Insurance: An Analysis* (Washington, D.C.: American Enterprise Institute, 1971); Martin Feldstein, "A New Approach to National Health Insurance," *Public Interest*, no. 23 (Spring 1971), pp. 93–105; Joseph Newhouse, Charles Phelps, and William Schwartz, "Policy Options and the Impact of National Health Insurance," *New England Journal of Medicine*, vol. 290, no. 24 (June 13, 1974), pp. 1345–1359; *Problems and Issues in National Health Insurance* (New York: Tax Foundation, 1974); and A. E. Ehrbar, "A Radical Prescription for Medical Care," *Fortune*, vol. 95 (February 1977), pp. 164–172.

mental system, it has many unfortunate consequences, especially in the long run.

We begin with a brief discussion of public health insurance, noting the various rationales for it and the variety of programs that have been discussed. Following that, we discuss in detail the nature of public insurance in private markets, and exactly where the complexities arise.

Chapter 3 presents the basic model. It shows that full coverage service benefits are incompatible with private provision of services. Using that as a starting point, various types of cost sharing are analyzed. Coinsured service benefits (insurance pays a proportion of costs) are shown to permit a stable equilibrium, but they increase prices for services, both through a subsidy effect and through a reduction of search activity and cost consciousness on the part of buyers. An alternative method of cost sharing is the use of indemnity benefits (fixed insurance payment per unit of service). It is shown that indemnity benefits are less inflationary than coinsured service benefits. This follows directly from the different nature of the subsidy and indirectly from the differential impact on search and cost consciousness. Finally, deductibles are assessed.

Chapter 4 deals with the regulation of fees and reimbursements. Fee regulation is essential to market provision of fully insured services, and can also be used in conjunction with cost-sharing insurance. We discuss fee schedules (fee is set by the insurer) and show how the results differ according to whether the provider is prohibited from making extra charges to the patient (sometimes called assignment). Surprisingly, when extra charges are allowed, the results for service benefits that are regulated are equivalent to indemnity benefits that are unregulated. The problem of determining the fee schedule is then considered.

One method of regulating fees is limitation to "usual, customary, and prevailing" levels. This introduces an element of market pricing into regulation, but only when part of the population is uninsured or cost sharing is important. With complete coverage of the entire population, automatic inflation results.

Chapter 5 discusses an alternative way of combining public insurance with private provision of services—HMOs. While HMOs have received wide attention as a potential solution to many health care problems, we do not believe that other writers have really isolated what is unique with this organizational innovation. In our analysis we suggest that market transactions between insurers and providers are particularly inefficient and that HMOs increase efficiency by combining the provider and insurer into one organization. They are thus a particularly useful vehicle for public financing of health care.

The concluding chapter discusses alternative forms of public insurance and the implications of this analysis for choices among them.

There are three appendixes. The first discusses the appropriateness of microeconomic analysis for examination of medical care issues. Recognizing the important differences between medical care and other goods and services, the section shows that the basic economic model is useful in analyzing the effects of various insurance and regulatory policies on medical care prices, output, and quality. For example, while a nonprofit hospital might produce a different array of services than a for-profit hospital, both should respond to increased demand for care by treating more patients and by providing more service-intensive care. The second and third appendixes present graphical and mathematical treatments respectively of the analyses in chapters 3 and 4.

2

The Problems of Public Payment and Private Provision

Financing privately provided health care through public insurance has certain predictable consequences for the amount, price, and quality of care the system produces. In previewing these, let us first consider the consequences various proponents of public insurance hope for, that is, their rationales for supporting public insurance. In addition, let us survey some of the forms of insurance proposed since, as will become clear in the course of this study, the consequences for amount, price, and quality of care depend heavily on the particular form of public insurance chosen for enactment. Isolation of the exact effects is particularly difficult because, as we also argue, there exists considerable monopoly among private providers of health care, dispersed though they may be in the economy.

It is increasingly common for governments of developed nations either to provide or to induce private organizations to provide insurance for medical expenditures.[1] In the United States, public insurance of the "direct provision" variety has been available to the elderly from the federal government since 1966. Also, substantial federal subsidies have induced states to provide insurance for the welfare population and "medical indigents." An issue that has been debated heatedly since the 1940s is whether the federal government should provide or arrange for health insurance for the rest of the population, that is, for national health insurance (NHI).

Rationales for Public Payment

A number of rationales for NHI have been put forward. The one most frequently mentioned stems from a concern for the health status of the

---

[1] Underdeveloped countries are more likely to provide the medical services directly through public clinics than to provide insurance to purchase medical care.

poor. Many speak of a "right" to medical care of all citizens, implying that it is a governmental responsibility to ensure that some care is available to all. One holder of this point of view is Senator Edward M. Kennedy:

> I believe good health care should be a right for all Americans. Health is so basic to man's ability to bring to fruition his opportunities as an American that each of us should guarantee the best possible health care to every American at a cost he can afford. Health care is not a luxury or an optional service we can do without.[2]

Kennedy advocates NHI to eliminate the financial barriers to medical care. Other writers also call for subsidizing health care for the poor, though they may use different terms in their arguments. According to Mark Pauly, for instance, "It is probably a common characteristic of human beings that they dislike seeing or knowing of other human beings who are suffering. When and if medical care prevents or alleviates known suffering, therefore, individuals other than the direct consumer may benefit."[3] These writers base NHI on a charitable instinct by the nonpoor and see a public program as an efficient way of carrying out this aim.[4]

The notion of a right to care and the charitable instinct toward the health status of the poor have similar policy implications. Both are used to argue that the government should provide subsidized care to the poor or that it should finance the private provision of care to this group. Some proponents of the right to care are more absolutist. They insist that the money price of care be zero. This view is not

---

[2] Edward M. Kennedy, *In Critical Condition* (New York: Simon and Schuster, 1972), p. 17. Other discussions of a right to care are found in the comments of Representative Bella Abzug of New York (p. 3006), Senator Thomas McIntyre of New Hampshire (p. 2828), and Senator Lee Metcalf of Montana (p. 1351) in U.S. Congress, House, Ways and Means Committee, *National Health Insurance Proposals*, 92nd Congress, 1st session, 1971. Governor Marvin Mandel of Maryland (p. 3537), Governor Phillip Noel of Rhode Island (p. 3551), and Representative Michael Harrington of Massachusetts (p. 1718) also discuss the issue in U.S. Congress, House, Ways and Means Committee, *National Health Insurance*, 94th Congress, 1st session, 1975. Also, see the comments of Senator Jacob Javits of New York (pp. 105–106) and Senator Claiborne Pell of Rhode Island (pp. 198–200) in U.S. Congress, Senate, Committee on Labor and Public Welfare, *National Health Insurance*, 91st Congress, 2nd session, 1970. Finally, see the comments of Leonard Woodcock, president of the United Auto Workers of America (pp. 102–110), and Whitney Young, director of the Urban League (pp. 258–259), in U.S. Congress, Senate, Committee on Labor and Public Welfare, Subcommittee on Health, *The Health Care Crisis*, 92nd Congress, 2nd session, 1972.

[3] Mark V. Pauly, *Medical Care at Public Expense* (New York: Praeger, 1971), pp. 9–10.

[4] Without a public program, some individuals may choose simply to enjoy the results of others' charity toward the poor and not contribute themselves.

necessarily a consequence of one's general political persuasion: interestingly, the People's Republic of China makes substantial use of consumer cost sharing in its health care system.[5]

A rationale closely related to the above is a desire to redistribute income to the poor. Some may support a negative income tax or a similar general income transfer, but find it easier politically to accomplish this goal through a series of programs subsidizing specific goods and services (food, housing, medical care). While it may not be politically acceptable to give additional income to the poor, it is often all right to give additional food, fuel oil, housing, and/or medical care. Thus some people who have no particular concern with medical care for the poor may advocate NHI as an indirect way of redistributing income.

A very different rationale concerns some of the problems that afflict private health insurance. All types of insurance are burdened with two inherent problems: moral hazard and adverse selection. Moral hazard is the effect of insurance in changing the insured's behavior so that the insured loss occurs more frequently and is of greater magnitude than would be the case without insurance. In health care, there is clearly an incentive for the insured consumer to utilize more medical care. Moral hazard affects both public and private insurance in the same manner, and the tools available to cope with it (discussed below) are the same for both.

Adverse selection is a tendency for high-risk persons to be more likely to purchase insurance than low-risk persons. Clearly, if one expects to use more than the average amount of medical services, owing either to poor health or to high taste for medical care, an insurance policy is more valuable. This leads to a preponderance of high-risk persons in an insurance pool which increases the premiums of all those insured. In health insurance, private insurers have responded to the adverse selection problem with group insurance. If insurance is purchased by all members of a group formed for some other purpose, such as for employment, then adverse selection can be avoided.[6] Also, groups that use less medical care than the average in the community

---

[5] See Chi-Pang Wen and Charles W. Hays, "Health Care Financing in China," *Medical Care*, vol. 14, no. 3 (March 1976), pp. 241–255, and Teh-We Hu, "The Financing and Economic Efficiency of Rural Health Services in the People's Republic of China," *International Journal of Health Services*, vol. 6, no. 2 (1976), pp. 239–250, for a fascinating look at the Communist Chinese system.

[6] In other types of insurance (such as life insurance), the problem is minimized by rating according to risk class. If the insurer knows as much about the probability of death as the insured (on the basis of age, sex, and physical examination), then adverse selection will not occur. The fact that this approach does not appear to be sufficient to minimize adverse selection in health insurance is testimony to the importance of tastes for medical care in determining utilization.

stand to gain by insurance rating based on their own experience. This factor, in conjunction with the administrative savings and tax advantages of employer-paid health insurance, accounts for the preponderance of group purchases of private health insurance in the United States.[7]

Insuring through employment groups has substantial benefits for those who are members of these groups but poses a problem for those who are not. The latter face premiums based on the experience of the residual pool of relatively high utilizers. Those who are not employed tend to be in worse health than those who are, as poor health often prevents employment. Adverse selection among those not in employee groups further raises the cost of health insurance for those in this category. The high cost of individual insurance leads some not to purchase health insurance at all, or to purchase only limited coverage.

Some advocate NHI as a means of avoiding the adverse selection problem and its concentrated effects on those who have not been able to use an employment group to obtain access to low-cost insurance. When insurance is mandatory, as in most NHI proposals, the adverse selection problem cannot exist. The Medicare and Medicaid programs single out people with poor access to insurance, owing both to lack of group membership and to low income, and provide tax-subsidized insurance. However, public provision of insurance is not necessary to deal with adverse selection, as private insurance could be made mandatory. This is a feature of some NHI proposals.

An additional problem in private health insurance markets is the fact that some consumers lack coverage for very large, catastrophic expenses. A recent report from the Tax Foundation says:

> Of all the problems related to operations of the health care system, perhaps the greatest amount of public concern has been caused by those spectacular instances where families, including some in middle and upper income brackets, have been forced into acute financial straits, at times even bankruptcy, by huge financial burdens resulting from severe prolonged catastrophic illness on the part of one of their members.[8]

But the situation is improving. Data from a survey by the Health Insurance Association of America show that major medical expense pro-

---

[7] In 1975, 86 percent of those insured by private insurance companies had group policies. *Source Book of Health Insurance Data, 1976–77* (New York: Health Insurance Institute, 1976), p. 23. On tax savings, see Bridger Mitchell and Ronald Vogel, "Health and Taxes: An Assessment of the Medical Deduction," *Southern Economic Journal*, vol. 41 (April 1975), pp. 660–672.

[8] *Problems and Issues in National Health Insurance*, pp. 15–16.

tection has been increasing rapidly over time. Insurance company major medical insurance protected 2.2 million persons against catastrophic expenses in 1954, 21.9 million in 1959, 47.3 million in 1964, 73.8 million in 1969, and 92.2 million in 1975. While maximum benefit limits are still included even in these policies, the situation is improving rapidly here too. In 1974, 56 percent of those with insurance company major medical coverage had maximum limits lower than $50,000, which exposes them to some catastrophic risk, especially in high medical cost areas, but in 1975 the proportion had fallen to 33 percent.[9] This occurs even though the additional premium required to eliminate limits altogether would apparently be small.

A number of explanations have been offered for low limits. It has been alleged that consumers have not been aware of the risks of large medical expenditures until recently, and thus have been unwilling to pay the extra premiums for catastrophic coverage. Howard Kunreuther argues that consumers have special difficulties in processing information regarding events of very low probability.[10] A related version of this explanation is that people would rather depend on public welfare systems and charity for this contingency. However, this would appear attractive only for those with limited savings.

Others have alleged a reluctance on the part of insurance companies to be exposed to these risks, assuming a difficulty in estimating them. However, it is hard to believe that this could persist in a competitive environment: the returns must surely be large for companies willing to experiment with new types of coverage desired by consumers. Insurer behavior cannot, therefore, be the cause of some consumers' lack of catastrophic coverage.

It is interesting to note how inexpensive complete catastrophic insurance would be. A study by Howard Birnbaum indicates that for noninstitutionalized persons under age sixty-five who had health care expenditures exceeding $5,000 in 1974, the out-of-pocket expense was only $1.1 billion—about $6 per person when spread over the noncatastrophically ill in this group.[11] Even allowing for administrative costs and any moral hazard of the added insurance, it is difficult to see how the cost of complete catastrophic coverage could exceed $10–15 per person annually.

---

[9] Source Book of Health Insurance Data, 1975–76, p. 28, 1976–77, p. 27.

[10] Howard Kunreuther, "Limited Knowledge and Insurance Protection," Public Policy, vol. 24, no. 2 (Spring 1976), pp. 227–261, and Richard Zeckhauser, "Coverage for Catastrophic Illness," Public Policy, vol. 21, no. 2 (Spring 1973), pp. 149–172.

[11] Howard Birnbaum, A National Profile of Catastrophic Illness, final report, National Center for Health Services Research, contract no. HRA 230-75-6141 (Cambridge, Mass.: Abt Associates, Inc., 1977).

Numerous statements by public officials and interest group spokespersons indicate that insurance for catastrophic expenses is something that they believe most people desire.[12] Thus, it is often a part of NHI proposals and in some cases, their cornerstone, as in the National Catastrophic Illness Protection Act of 1973 (Roe-Beall) and the Catastrophic Health Insurance and Medical Assistance Reform Act (Long-Ribicoff).

A final major reason for the advocacy of public insurance by some is a desire to obtain a vehicle for government reform of the health care system. A number of instruments for change are included in many NHI proposals. One is the requirement of government approval of all construction of health facilities and purchases of major equipment. Another is the use of prospective reimbursement in paying hospitals for their services in place of the cost reimbursement used by many Blue Cross plans, Medicare, and Medicaid. Some plans give financial encouragement to the development of health maintenance organizations (HMOs).

While advocates of these methods of government intervention may support NHI as a way to introduce them, they appear to see it only as an expedient. While NHI is a sufficient condition for extensive regulation, it clearly is not a necessary one. In certain states, all the regulatory powers envisioned in NHI proposals are already in place. Most states have passed certificate of need laws, requiring approval of major construction and equipment purchases before a new facility can be licensed. Recent federal legislation requires certificate of need approval of capital expenditures for future Medicaid and Medicare re-

---

[12] See the comments of Senator Lloyd Bentsen of Texas (pp. 135–138), Public Citizens' Health Group of the District of Columbia (pp. 50, 53–57), and the Special Committee on National Health Care Needs (pp. 113–118) in U.S. Congress, House, Ways and Means Committee, Subcommittee on Health, *Health Insurance for the Unemployed and Related Legislation*, 94th Congress, 1st session, 1975. U.S. Congress, Senate, Committee on Labor and Public Welfare, Subcommittee on Health, *A Report: Medical Care Systems in Foreign Countries*, 93rd Congress, 2nd session, 1974, chap. 3, pp. 30–44, also deals with the desire for catastrophic insurance coverage. Medical catastrophies and the poor are discussed by Whitney Young, director of the Urban League, in U.S. Congress, Senate, Committee on Labor and Public Welfare, *National Health Care*, 91st Congress, 2nd session, 1970, pp. 253–260. Senator Jacob Javits has often expressed the view that catastrophic insurance must be assured before a more comprehensive plan is developed, for example in U.S. Congress, Senate, Committee on Labor and Public Welfare, Subcommittee on Health, *The Health Care Crisis*, 92nd Congress, 2nd session, 1972, pp. 1551–1553. See the comments of Senator Abraham Ribicoff of Connecticut (p. 777) and Senator William Brock of Tennessee (p. 3461) in the same hearings. However, in U.S. Congress, House, Ways and Means Committee, *National Health Insurance*, 93rd Congress, 2nd session, 1974, Representative Bella Abzug (p. 3486) and Senator Edward Kennedy (p. 3515) argue that catastrophic insurance problems must be dealt with in a comprehensive plan for national health insurance.

imbursement, making such regulation effectively universal. A smaller number of states have hospital rate-setting commissions. Indeed, the federal government controlled health care prices from 1971 to 1974 as part of the Economic Stabilization Program, despite the absence of NHI. President Carter has introduced legislation putting a ceiling on capital expenditures that can be approved under the certificate of need process and requiring federal regulation of hospital revenues (the latter similar to that developed at the end of the Economic Stabilization Program).[13] On the subject of HMOS, the federal government provides limited start-up grants and requires employers who provide health insurance to their employees to offer HMO membership as an option. The government is also active in the field of health manpower: training is subsidized and medical schools must ensure that a certain proportion of their graduates choose primary care.

More extensive government control of medical care that requires NHI (such as budgeting expenditures for areas and/or individual providers) can be imagined. However, with the notable exception of the Health Security proposal, none of the NHI bills envisions such controls. Consequently, we do not consider reorganization of the health care system to be a serious rationale for NHI.

Types of NHI Programs

There is an indefinitely large set of potential variations in NHI programs. Variation is possible in who is covered, what services are covered, the extent and type of cost sharing, the method of reimbursing providers, the method of financing, and the division of responsibility between the public and private sectors.[14] While it is not the purpose of this study to elaborate on all these dimensions of public insurance, some are relevant to our analysis of the interaction between public insurance and private provision of services. Particularly important are the dimensions of population coverage and cost sharing and the methods of providing insurance and paying providers.

A crucial dimension in public insurance for privately provided care is the proportion of the population covered. Two approaches are commonly suggested. One is to cover only those segments of the population that one considers either to be medically underserved or in danger of impoverishment should a serious illness occur. This has been the approach taken by the United States thus far in providing health

---

[13] Hospital Cost Containment Act of 1977 (S 1391, HR 6575).

[14] See Karen Davis, *National Health Insurance: Benefits, Costs, and Consequences* (Washington, D.C.: Brookings Institution, 1975), pp. 56–79, for an extensive discussion of these issues.

11

insurance for the elderly (Medicare) and the poor (Medicaid). The approach would be continued by certain NHI proposals that would expand Medicaid coverage to more of the poor and reform many aspects of it. The alternative approach is coverage of the entire population. This is common in Western Europe and is the approach taken in the majority of NHI proposals in the United States.[15]

While the decision whether to cover all or part of the population involves many practical and philosophical issues, the issues of particular importance here concern the operation of a market with two segments of buyers (private and public) but one segment of sellers, as contrasted with a market where all buyers are publicly insured. In the former arrangement, the uninsured or privately insured market can be used as a guide for payment rates in the publicly insured market, although the private market in turn is influenced by policies of the public insurer. The private market provides valuable, if imperfect, signals because of competition for the relatively informed and cost-conscious private patients. Thus, private market prices would provide a crude but useful guide for public policy. When all buyers are completely publicly financed, such market signals would be eliminated, making efficiency in the design of a reimbursement system very difficult. The higher the proportion of the population covered by public insurance, the more important and the more difficult reimbursement policy becomes.

A hotly debated issue is the extent to which patients should contribute directly (rather than indirectly as taxpayers) to the cost of their care purchased under NHI. Most but not all proposals include cost sharing of one type or another, either a deductible scheme, a coinsurance scheme, or indemnity limit. Under a deductible scheme, the patient pays the first dollars of costs incurred during a given period of time. Advantages of deductibles are that they can reduce administrative costs and moral hazard for those people who do not exceed them. In addition, they cause a portion of medical care to be purchased under market incentives, thus diluting the effect of public insurance on price and output.

Under a coinsurance scheme, the patient pays a proportion of the cost of services. This also restores some incentive to the purchaser to seek lower priced services and some incentive to suppliers to compete on the basis of price. Coinsurance reduces the increase in price and quantity resulting from the insurance benefits. Under the third form of cost sharing, indemnity insurance, the insurance provides a fixed number

---

[15] See Alan Maynard, *Health Care in the European Economic Community* (London: Croom, Helm, 1975); and U.S. Department of Health, Education, and Welfare, *National Health Insurance Proposals*, 1974.

of dollars per unit of services. The patient is left to pay the difference between that and the price.[16]

Regardless of the particular form, cost sharing reduces wasteful spending from the subsidy effect of health insurance. It also makes possible some role for the decentralized market in the provision of health insurance. However, if not properly designed, cost sharing can defeat some of the prime goals of NHI—increased use of care by the poor and protection against catastrophic expenses.

Some proposals for NHI have provisions to encourage HMOs. The decision whether services are to be provided to the insured by HMOs or by fee-for-service practitioners should have a substantial impact on the utilization of medical care and its price. However, we postpone discussion of this issue until chapter 5.

The method of providing insurance may have impacts on the market for medical services. Government may provide the insurance directly (as in Medicare), may require employers and/or individuals to purchase private insurance, or may subsidize private insurance. The relevance of this choice for our discussion depends upon the extent of public regulation of the required or subsidized private insurance.

If private insurance policies are required to be carbon copies of government insurance with little scope for cost control through benefit design or administrative controls, then there can be virtually no difference in effects on the medical care market. If regulations are looser, then there will be incentives for insurers to seek out a benefit structure and administrative controls that reduce utilization and lower prices. However, there is no incentive to private insurers to seek to minimize *average* price increases, since these benefits are spread over all insurers. Indeed, if a single insurer offers a more restrictive fee schedule than others and providers cannot charge the patient, then its policyholders are likely to have trouble obtaining medical care. However potentially important the possibilities of administrative cost controls by competing private insurers may be, we must ignore them in our discussion because they are simply outside the scope of this study.[17]

---

[16] The patient usually is not permitted to profit from paying a price lower than the indemnity payment.

[17] For more on the role of competing private health insurers in controlling costs through administrative controls, see Clark C. Havighurst, "Controlling Health Care Costs: Strengthening the Private Sector's Hand," *Journal of Health Politics, Policy and Law*, vol. 1, no. 4 (Winter 1977), pp. 471–498. A fascinating description of the actual cost control mechanisms used by private health insurers before organized medicine created Oregon Blue Shield to eliminate the practices is contained in Lawrence Goldberg and Warren Greenberg, "The Effect of Physician-Controlled Health Insurance: U.S. v. Oregon State Medical Society," *Journal of Health Politics, Policy and Law*, vol. 2, no. 1 (Spring 1977), pp. 48–78.

The method by which providers are paid is a crucial dimension of any public insurance program, though it has received little attention thus far. Reimbursements can take a number of forms. Providers may be paid according to a fee schedule, with a set reimbursement for a given service and payments that are uniform for all providers. Another method is "usual, customary, and prevailing" reimbursement, under which each provider receives a fee based on rates charged to private patients, but limited to a ceiling based on rates prevailing in the area. This contrasts with fee schedules in that, first, different providers may be paid different rates for the same service depending on their fees to private patients and the area in which they are located, and second, there is less discretion for government officials in setting rates. Once "prevailing" is defined (usually by selecting a percentile in the distribution of fees), the reimbursement payments are automatically determined.

Aside from the choice of fee schedule or limitations to usual, customary, and prevailing fees, there is still another issue. Are providers permitted to charge the patients extra fees or is the public reimbursement to be considered full payment? If the latter, the provider is said to accept assignment. These issues are considered below in the analysis of regulation.

Public Insurance in Private Markets

The essential characteristic of public insurance in private markets is that the government does not have direct control over the output or, in some cases, over the price of medical care. Thus, the government can set the type and extent of benefits for its insurance and possibly the price. But, the private market then determines the total quantity and composition of services and therefore total expenditures on medical care. This sort of arrangement is common. For example, West Germany, Sweden, France, and the Netherlands have such plans; the American Medicare and Medicaid programs are also of this type.[18]

For the centralized national health care plans, an examination of the government's policies and the size of the budget suffices for estimating expected annual costs, even if the actual level, distribution, and amount of care provided is unclear. But, for public insurance in private markets, the government's plan (that is, its insurance packages and price controls, if any) are only a very small part of the story. To know the impacts of such programs, one must be able to analyze the response

[18] William A. Glaser, *Paying the Doctor: Systems of Remuneration and Their Effects* (Baltimore: The Johns Hopkins University Press, 1970).

14

of the private market to the government insurance policies. This requires the use of economic analysis. For any given plan, one would like to know what the resulting total expenditures on medical care will be, that is, what the total output of medical care and its price will be.

There has been a great deal of useful analysis of the role of health insurance in raising the demand for health services.[19] However, these studies examine exclusively the behavior of consumers when faced with differing insurance benefits and medical prices. They do not consider the response of providers to the altered behavior of consumers. Thus, such studies cannot be used to predict reliably the total reaction of the health care system to the imposition of NHI. The most important missing element in these analyses is recognition of the monopoly power of suppliers. As we argue in chapter 3, provider monopoly power increases with more complete insurance coverage, and this has especially important consequences for the effects of increased insurance coverage.

When elements of monopoly exist, analysis of various NHI schemes is more complex. For instance, when examining the response of a competitive market, the type of insurance does not matter. In fact, many of the available empirical demand studies do not differentiate according to type of insurance.[20] But under an NHI scheme, if one considers a given output of medical care, the market price that results depends not only on the amount of insurance but also on the type. Alternatively, for a given expenditure of government funds on public insurance, the resulting quantity of health care actually supplied to consumers depends on the type of insurance.

Even if the degree of monopoly power of the providers is constant, the analysis would still be complex. But there is an additional factor that reinforces the effect of different types of health insurance on prices and outputs. The major cause of the monopoly power is consumer ignorance and/or indifference. As we shall see, certain types of in-

---

[19] See Paul B. Ginsburg and Lawrence M. Manheim, "Insurance Copayment and Health Services Utilization," *Journal of Economics and Business*, vol. 25 (Spring-Summer 1973), pp. 142–153; Martin S. Feldstein, "Hospital Cost Inflation: A Study of Nonprofit Price Dynamics," *American Economic Review*, vol. 61 (December 1971), pp. 853–872; Joseph P. Newhouse and Charles E. Phelps, "New Estimates of Price and Income Elasticities of Medical Care Services," in Richard N. Rosett, ed., *The Role of Health Insurance in the Health Services Sector* (New York: National Bureau of Economic Research, 1976), pp. 261–312; and Martin Feldstein and Amy Taylor, *The Rapid Rise of Hospital Costs* (Washington, D.C.: Executive Office of the President, Council on Wage and Price Stability, staff report, January 1977).

[20] For example, Richard N. Rosett and Lien Fu Huang, "The Effect of Health Insurance on the Demand for Medical Care," *Journal of Political Economy*, vol. 81 (March-April 1973), pp. 281–305, and Feldstein, "Hospital Cost Inflation."

surance reduce consumer incentives for information gathering and make consumers more indifferent to cost differences. This will in itself increase the extent of monopoly power and therefore raise prices and lower output. Analysis of such important subtleties is a major goal of this monograph.

3

Copayment: A Vital Component of Public Insurance

Different types of insurance have different effects on medical care markets. Complete insurance effectively destroys the market allocation of care—price tends to rise explosively and the introduction of consumer copayment is vital to restoring equilibrium. But, the form of the copayment has important effects on the prices paid and on the extent of monopoly power exercised by providers, even if we fix the proportion of the costs that we wish insurance to pay. Insurance that pays a fixed amount per unit of service (indemnity insurance) is superior to insurance that pays a fixed proportion of the costs (coinsured service benefits) in most of its effects. This chapter presents the analysis of the effect of the various forms of insurance, but first let us examine briefly the setting for which we have reached the above conclusions.

The Medical Market: Incentives, Feedback, and Units of Service

The Incentive Problem with Health Insurance. Public insurance that relies on private markets for the supply of the medical care subsidizes medical care. That is, the insurance contract provides payment contingent on the use of medical care, not contingent on becoming ill, and it also lowers the price to the consumer of additional units of consumption. As a result of facing lower prices, consumers demand more medical care, thus raising both quantity and price of medical care. These responses, as we have discussed above, are called moral hazard.[1]

---

[1] The subsidy problem is a special case of the general problem of moral hazard in insurance. For a more complete discussion, see H. E. Frech III, "The Regulation of Health Insurance," Ph.D. dissertation, University of California, Los Angeles, 1974, pp. 5–18; Isaac Ehrlich and Gary S. Becker, "Market Insurance, Self-Insurance and Self-Protection," *Journal of Political Economy*, vol. 80, no. 4 (July-August, 1972), pp. 623–648; and John M. Marshall, "Moral Hazard," working paper in economics, no. 18, University of California, Santa Barbara, May 1974.

The demand increase brought about by the subsidy inherent in health insurance can be reduced by administrative limitations on prices and consumer spending. For example, the insurer might review claims and refuse to pay those thought to be excessive for the diagnosis. Or, prior approval of surgery might be required, perhaps involving concurrence of more than one physician. However, owing to the opposition of organized medicine, the use of such potentially powerful administrative controls by both private insurers and the government is quite restricted and will be ignored in what follows.[2] Even though administrative monitoring and cost controls are of some importance in existing private health insurance and seem to have great potential, it would require a separate study to do them justice.

An important form of insurance is provided through the health maintenance organization (HMO), of which the prepaid group practice form is most common. In these plans, the insurer and the provider are combined so that medical care is rationed by close administrative monitoring. This is discussed in detail in chapter 5.

Feedback System. In ordinary private health insurance there is feedback from the impact of the insurance to the type of insurance offered and its prices. If a given type of insurance leads to very large consumer expenditures, the insurer will charge higher premiums for it and face a decline in the number of policies sold. To analyze private insurance, such feedback must be considered because it affects individual and group choices of insurance.[3]

For our analysis we can ignore feedback and assume that the form of the insurance is fixed. This is a reasonable assumption for two reasons. First, most national health insurance plans contemplated provide for little consumer choice. There is either a defined benefit package or a floor under which benefit structures in private policies may not go. Second, the government does not have as strong an incentive to react to high costs as does a private insurer. Historically, government insurance programs have not changed a great deal as a result of adverse

---

[2] Testimony of Clark C. Havighurst, in U.S. Congress, Senate, Committee on the Judiciary, Subcommittee on Antitrust and Monopoly, *Hearings on Competition in the Health Services Market*, 93rd Congress, 2nd session, May 14, 15, 17, 29, 30, and July 10, 1974, pp. 1074–1076. See also Clark C. Havighurst, "Controlling Health Care Costs: Strengthening the Private Sector's Hand," *Journal of Health Politics, Policy and Law*, vol. 1, no. 4 (Winter 1977), pp. 478–482, and Lawrence Goldberg and Warren Greenberg, "The Effect of Physician-Controlled Health Insurance: U.S. v. Oregon State Medical Society," *Journal of Health Politics, Policy and Law*, vol. 2, no. 1 (Spring 1977), pp. 48–60.

[3] Frech, "Health Insurance," pp. 19–36, and Joseph P. Newhouse and Charles E. Phelps, *On Having Your Cake and Eating It Too: Econometric Problems in Estimating the Demand for Health Services* (Santa Monica: Rand, 1974).

experience, as Medicaid and Medicare illustrate. In the eight years from 1967 to 1975 Medicaid expenditures grew from $2.5 to $13.0 billion and Medicare expenditures from $3.4 to $14.8 billion,[4] but this dramatic overrun has not led to important increases in consumer out-of-pocket payments. Only minor regulation has been tried, but with little effect.[5]

The Basic Unit of Medical Care. Most of our analysis is conducted in terms of units of "medical care," which is used as a composite of all the different types of medical care. Further, the analysis is largely concerned with "pure" medical care, isolated from other dimensions such as waiting time, quality, location, attractiveness of surroundings, hours of service, and so on. While this degree of abstraction is easier to achieve conceptually than in practice (especially for quality), it is useful in that it allows us to define demand and supply for a good (medical care) defined in standard units. Further, this approach meshes with the usual treatment in both health insurance and in fee regulation, which also define care in terms of physical procedures.

A Monopoly Model of Medical Providers

Health care is provided by a wide variety of sources, including hospitals and nursing homes, both proprietary and nonprofit, independent physicians, groups of physicians, and home health workers. We cannot develop a separate model of behavior for each type of provider without adding more confusion than light to the analysis. Instead, we focus on independent physicians and argue that the analysis applies in an approximate sense to all other providers. Three reasons suggest focusing on the physician. First, physicians are the decision makers of the medical care system, exercising influence beyond their practices.

---

[4] U.S. Department of Commerce, *Statistical Abstract of the U.S.* (Washington, D.C.: Government Printing Office, various years).

[5] See David Salkever and Thomas Bice, "The Effect of Certificate-of-Need Laws on Hospital Investments," *Milbank Memorial Fund Quarterly: Health and Society*, vol. 55 (Spring 1977), pp. 185–214, and J. Joel May, "The Impact of Health Planning," Graduate Program in Hospital Administration, University of Chicago, 1973 (mimeographed), for recent results on supply limitation. See also Clifton Gaus and Fred Hellinger, "Results of Hospital Prospective Reimbursement in the U.S.," paper presented to the International Conference on Policies for the Containment of Health Care Costs and Expenditures, The John E. Fogarty International Center, Bethesda, Maryland, June 3, 1976, which reviews studies on prospective reimbursement. For a study of hospital regulation under the Economic Stabilization Program, see Paul B. Ginsburg, "Impact of the Economic Stabilization Program on Hospital Costs: An Analysis with Aggregate Data," in Michael Zubkoff, Ira Raskin, and Ruth Hanft, eds., *Hospital Cost Containment: Selected Notes for Future Policy* (New York: Milbank Memorial Fund, 1978), pp. 293–323.

Second, physician services will experience the largest increase in coverage under most NHI proposals. Finally, qualitative analysis has shown that the response of other providers to changes in insurance and regulations is often identical to that of physicians. These points are discussed in more detail in Appendix A.

Monopoly Caused by Imperfect Information. We take the view that medical care is provided monopolistically. The monopoly does not arise from the usual cause of a small number of sellers: even reasonably small cities usually contain several hospitals and scores of physicians. The monopoly problem arises because of the extremely poor and costly information available to medical consumers.

Since consumers are not well aware of price, attractiveness, and quality for the many alternative sources of medical care, each provider has something of a "captive market." If he were to raise his price somewhat, some but *not all* of his customers would desert him. On the other hand, if he were to lower his price, he would gain some customers but not the large number required to induce competitive behavior. The supplier does not have a complete monopoly since some consumers will seek other sources in response to higher prices. Technically, the situation is best described as monopolistic or imperfectly competitive.

Consumers' poor information about alternatives arises from several factors. First, medical services themselves are complex and highly varied, making it difficult for consumers to decide which alternatives are comparable. Second, regulators and organized physicians have tended to reduce information flows (for example by banning advertising).[6] Some such restrictions are currently under antitrust attack because of their tendency to increase monopoly power. Third, common types of health insurance reduce consumer concern about costs and incentive to search. This is examined in more detail below.

To analyze all these impacts on the monopoly power of providers would be extremely complex. Therefore, we conduct our analysis in terms of a simple monopoly model, which captures the essential flavor of provider behavior.

The Initial Situation: Demand without Insurance. The starting point of the analysis is a hypothetical situation where consumers have no

---

[6] For more on regulatory and professional restrictions on consumer information, see H. E. Frech III, "Regulatory Reform: The Case of the Medical Care Industry," in Thomas G. Moore, ed., *Regulatory Reform* (Washington, D.C.: American Enterprise Institute, forthcoming).

insurance.[7] Since the great majority of consumers do have some form of government or private insurance,[8] this no-insurance demand curve is not observed in the market. However, its use enables us to isolate the impact of NHI without becoming involved in complex problems of how the new public insurance partially substitutes for existing private insurance.[9]

Impacts of Service Benefits

Service benefits are defined as benefits that reimburse consumers for a proportion of their health care bills. This is distinguishable from the major alternative, indemnity insurance, which reimburses consumers a fixed dollar amount per unit of service consumed. For example, service benefits might pay 80 percent of a hospital bill, while indemnity insurance provides $135 per hospital day. The reader should note that the term "service benefits" is sometimes used differently by other authors.

Complete Insurance: The Explosive Case. If service benefit insurance were enacted, very different results would occur if the insurance were complete, reimbursing 100 percent of medical expenses, rather than paying a proportion. Much current hospital insurance (for example, most Blue Cross, Medicare, Medicaid) is of this type. With complete insurance, the consumer bears none of the cost of services and there-

---

[7] For simplicity, we assume that there are no income or wealth effects on the demand for health care. See Marshall, "Moral Hazard," on wealth effects and health insurance.

[8] In 1974, 79.9 percent of the under-65 population had private hospital insurance, while 62.3 percent had private insurance for physician office and home visits. See Marjorie Smith Mueller and Paula A. Piro, "Private Health Insurance in 1974: A Review of Coverage, Enrollment and Financial Experience," *Social Security Bulletin*, vol. 39 (March 1976), pp. 3–20. All the over-65 population is covered by Medicare. While there are no data on the number of people that are covered by Medicaid, 1970 survey data showed that 4 percent of the population had received Medicaid benefits of some kind. See Charles Phelps, "Effects of Insurance on Demand for Medical Care," in Ronald Andersen, Joanna Kravits, and Odin Anderson, eds., *Equity in Health Services: Empirical Analysis in Social Policy* (Cambridge, Mass.: Ballinger, 1975), pp. 105–130.

[9] A public subsidy-in-kind for a privately supplied good can lead to some counterintuitive effects. For example, Peltzman found that the subsidy-in-kind provided by public higher education actually *reduced* the total expenditure on higher education in comparison with a situation where there was no subsidy. See Sam Peltzman, "The Effect of Government Subsidies-in-Kind on Private Expenditures: The Case of Higher Education," *Journal of Political Economy*, vol. 81, no. 1 (January-February 1973), pp. 1–28. For an analysis of a public subsidy-in-kind's increasing consumption of a good, see Kenneth Clarkson, *Food Stamps and Nutrition* (Washington, D.C.: American Enterprise Institute, 1975), pp. 65–69.

fore the price of services is irrelevant to him. (Remember, we are ignoring feedback through higher taxes or premiums to finance the cost of services. These feedback effects would be important for private insurers because they have a profit incentive to avoid wasteful benefit structures.) The consumer will demand the best possible care regardless of its cost, even when he views this care as only slightly more valuable than less costly care. The quantity of services he will demand is also clear—all the care with the slightest value to him. The individual consumer may reach this point of saturation after consuming a finite quantity of medical care, but the actual market outcome is not at all clear.

Full coverage insurance for all consumers is incompatible with market pricing and resource allocation. Nothing limits the prices charged by the suppliers of the insured services: suppliers can always gain by charging a higher price because the higher price does not discourage consumers who are indifferent to price. With no limit to the price, this is an explosive case. Such a plan would lead to disaster so quickly that it would not even be proposed without some formal or informal price regulation, which is discussed below. Put simply, complete insurance is not possible without extensive government control, which means that it is not compatible with the use of decentralized markets in providing insured health care.

Coinsurance: A Stable Equilibrium. Alternatively, service benefit insurance may be less than complete. This commonly observed type of benefit is often called coinsured service benefits or simply coinsurance and is illustrated by private major medical insurance policies. (Medicare Part B coverage pays 80 percent of outpatient fees, but the federal payment applies only up to a fee schedule—making this a better example of the regulated service benefits discussed in chapter 4.) The percentage the consumer pays is called the coinsurance rate. Requiring a proportional payment from the consumer induces him to consider price and total cost in his decisions, thus preserving the possibility of decentralized market pricing and resource allocation. Further, even if the price is centrally controlled, requiring a proportional consumer payment reduces the market pressure that regulations must contain.

However, coinsured service benefits will cause both price and quantity to rise relative to the no-insurance case. This occurs because the insurance reduces the price of medical care to consumers, thus inducing an increase in their demand for medical care. Unfortunately, the extra units of medical care consumed are worth less to the consumer than they cost to produce. For example, if the coinsurance rate were 20 percent, as it commonly is, a unit of medical care might cost

$10 to produce, but would be demanded by a consumer even if it were worth only $2 since this is all he must pay; $8 is wasted. This is the moral hazard cost (or welfare loss or waste) of health insurance. In a private competitive market, the buyer has a choice of more complete insurance at a higher price. In such a market, the individual or group balances the benefits of more complete insurance (greater security) against the inefficiency (moral hazard) reflected in higher premiums. In a public system, the government must balance security against inefficiency for all of us in designing a benefit structure.[10]

Service Benefits and Search Incentives: A Key to Monopoly Power. When one takes account of the fact that the suppliers of medical care are not complete monopolists but are rather incompletely competitive, some interesting new results emerge. The degree of competition among providers depends on the extent of consumer information about the price and attractiveness of care and on how concerned consumers are about differences. Clearly, if consumers are totally ignorant and cannot learn about prices of alternative sellers, the provider has a monopoly. For various reasons, the collection of information about medical prices and quality is costly. Rational consumers will search up to the point where the expected gains from search in lower prices are equal to the costs of search. Even if informed, they will not switch providers if they gain little of the savings.

Because service benefits pay part of the cost of care, the consumer gets only a part of the benefit of lower prices, generally a fairly small part. When a proportion of the cost of the service is not borne by the consumer, the benefits of search and of changing providers are proportionally reduced. For example, with a 10 percent coinsurance rate, a reduction in price from $90 to $80 gains only $1 for the consumer, rather than the $10 he would have enjoyed in the absence of

---

[10] There has been one attempt to measure empirically the welfare losses attributable to excess health insurance, that of Martin Feldstein in "The Welfare Loss of Excess Health Insurance," *Journal of Political Economy*, vol. 81, no. 2 (March-April 1973), pp. 251–280. However, there are serious problems with this approach. The loss is measured in the space defined by the price and quantity of medical care, rather than that of the price and quantity of health insurance. This necessitates an arbitrary treatment of the risk-spreading welfare gain aspect of the excess insurance. Further, the actual approach examines risk in financial terms only. This leads to the bizarre result that risk would be reduced if the price of medical care were to rise enough so that no one would demand medical care. It would seem that the basis of a measure of the welfare loss of excess health insurance should be the demand curve for health insurance. For a theoretical analysis of the problem of balancing the losses arising from the bad incentives of health insurance against the gains from risk reduction, see Richard Zeckhauser, "Medical Insurance: A Case Study of the Tradeoff between Risk Spreading and Appropriate Incentives," *Journal of Economic Theory*, vol. 2 (March 1970), pp. 10–26.

insurance. With almost no change in the costs of search, this disincentive effect will reduce the extent of consumer search and information-gathering activity of all kinds.[11] And even when informed, consumers will be less sensitive to price differences.

It is interesting to note that search for quality differences in alternative providers will also be suppressed by the disincentives inherent in coinsured service benefits. The impact on quality search derives from the more obvious impact on price search. When price searching, the consumer must also search on quality to be sure that the low-price providers he finds are of acceptable quality. Thus, the consumer actually considers both price and quality, seeking the favored price/quality combination.

As a result of service benefits, there is a diminution in consumer information and incentives concerning alternatives that causes a change in the monopoly power of the individual suppliers of medical care. Providers will find that less consumer information leads to greater incentive to raise prices—that is, more monopoly power.[12] When compared with the no-insurance case, coinsured service benefits will increase the degree of monopoly power. This will lead to higher prices and a smaller output rise than an analysis ignoring the information-and-indifference factor would suggest.[13] Under service benefits consumers are less informed of alternative providers, less willing to search for new providers in response to a price increase, and less willing to switch to a new provider who reduces price. As a result of this consumer "stickiness," providers can charge higher prices without appreciable loss of business. Nearly complete insurance is probably an important cause of the existing monopoly power of individual suppliers. A large majority of consumers have either complete or coinsured serv-

---

[11] Actually, coinsurance slightly reduces the cost of search if it reduces the out-of-pocket cost of the consumer's initial encounter with a new provider (for example, by paying a proportion of the cost of taking a medical history). However, many insurance plans refuse to pay for second opinions on surgery, which are a form of price searching as well as quality searching. Most of the search and information-gathering activity of consumers does not involve insurance payments.

[12] An additional cause of poor consumer information and thus greater provider monopoly power is the activity of organized medicine, such as prohibiting price advertising, which unfortunately is supported by many regulations. This appears to be an area where much of the regulation is designed to benefit the regulated providers. See Frech, "Regulatory Reform," and Lee Benham, "Guilds and the Form of Competition in the Health Care Sector," in Warren Greenberg, ed., *Competition in the Health Care Sector: Past, Present, and Future* (Washington, D.C.: Bureau of Economics, Federal Trade Commission, 1978), pp. 453–467.

[13] For an analysis of the impact of consumer information on the elasticity of demand facing a firm, see Phillip Nelson, "The Economic Consequences of Advertising," *Journal of Business*, vol. 48, no. 2 (April 1975), pp. 218–227.

ice benefits. Indeed, Mark Pauly believes, "The crucial fact is that at present uninsured persons, even though few in number, may be the only constraint on what costly procedures are done in hospitals. Remove this constraint and costs may flow ever upward, and at an increasing rate."[14] As long as hospitals depend partly on uninsured and incompletely insured patients, their better incentives will restrain price and cost for the entire medical care sector.

Service Mix: The Costliness of Care. The consequences of coinsured service benefits on the quantity and price of medical care consumed are serious indeed. But, the effects of this type of insurance in distorting the mixture of services consumed are probably even more striking and are probably responsible for more waste in the allocation of resources. This is a fairly complicated problem because the monopoly power of providers, as well as the coinsured service benefit type of insurance, distorts the mixture of services.[15] We will simplify a bit.

The bias to high quality, expensive services. Service benefits subsidize expenditures on higher quality and more pleasant medical care in a way analogous to the subsidy described above to higher quantity of medical care. An important element of quality is the variety of services available. Even if a more expensive physician or hospital provides only slightly higher quality (or more pleasant, or perhaps better located services), the consumer may be led by service benefits to purchase the higher cost care. For example, if the consumer's preferred provider is worth only $2 more in his eyes but costs $20 more, economic efficiency dictates that he choose the less attractive hospital. However, the rational decision given service benefits with 10 percent coinsurance is to choose the higher quality care.

For those consumers with complete coverage, the bias toward preferred types of care is limitless—such consumers will always prefer the very best of everything—even if the cost is great and the benefits small. Imagine auto insurance that paid the full cost of replacing a destroyed car with no limit on the type of car chosen—this will give an insight

---

[14] Mark V. Pauly, "Health Insurance and Hospital Behavior," in Cotton M. Lindsay, ed., *New Directions in Public Health Care: An Evaluation of Proposals for National Health Insurance* (San Francisco: Institute for Contemporary Studies, 1976), p. 113.

[15] The impact of monopoly on quality is quite subtle: it depends on how the slope of the demand curve changes in response to a quality change. See A. Michael Spence, "Monopoly, Quality and Regulation," *Bell Journal of Economics*, vol. 6, no. 2 (Autumn 1975), pp. 417–429.

into why American medicine is often described as "Cadillac medicine."[16]

There are also distortions in the service mix that are not related to the quality or attractiveness of different methods of treatment or different institutions for a given illness. The service mix in general is distorted because of the combination of monopoly power, the impact of coinsured service benefits, and differing price sensitivities for different services.

Distortion in service mix. Bias in services owing to service benefits is both predictable and perverse. Service benefits lead to a relatively larger increase in the quantity supplied of those services whose demand is more price-sensitive.[17] This occurs because an insurance subsidy encourages a greater increase in quantity demanded if the demand is more price-responsive. One might not be surprised to find visits for acne increasing while examinations for venereal disease remain constant under service benefits. Thus, the coinsured service mix is weighted in favor of what are probably the less important services, those that are most price-sensitive.

Impacts of Indemnity Benefits

Indemnity benefits have impacts quite different from service benefits in several respects. Some of the differences between indemnity and coinsured service benefits depend on the monopolistic nature of the supply of medical care and some do not.

Indemnity Benefits versus Coinsured Service Benefits. As we shall see, indemnity benefits raise price and quantity when compared with the initial no-insurance situation. Less obviously, indemnity leads to a lower price and a higher quantity of medical care than coinsurance. But, before the analysis, it is worthwhile to repeat the distinction between the terms "service benefit" and "indemnity benefit," as they are used in this paper. With service benefits, the insurer pays a percentage of the costs of medical care (which may be 100 percent). If indemnity benefits are provided, the insurer pays a fixed dollar amount per unit of

---

[16] For more on this see Martin S. Feldstein, *The Rising Cost of Hospital Care* (Washington, D.C.: Information Resources Press, 1971), pp. 32–35; Feldstein, "Hospital Cost Inflation," pp. 854–855; and Martin Feldstein and Amy Taylor, *The Rapid Rise of Hospital Costs* (Washington, D.C.: Executive Office of the President, Council on Wage and Price Stability, staff report, January 1977), pp. 29–38.

[17] For a mathematical demonstration of the dependence of product mix on coinsurance, see Appendix C.

services. Slightly less common in private health insurance than co-insured service benefits, indemnity insurance is usual with Blue Shield physician insurance, most commercial hospital insurance, and a minority of Blue Cross hospital insurance packages.

Let us examine the impact of this type of insurance on the demand for health services. First, it is important to note that there is no possibility of an explosive medical price increase with indemnity insurance. To see this, suppose that NHI with very high indemnity levels were enacted. As indemnity benefits are usually defined, the consumer cannot keep the savings if he finds health care for less than the indemnity payment. If the indemnity payment is $150 for a given service and the consumer finds the service for $135, he does not pocket the $15 savings. Because the indemnity insurer pays all costs per unit of service up to a limit, the consumer will ignore price as long as it is lower than the payment levels. As a consequence, the provider will naturally raise prices to the level of the allowable payments. However, further price increases will meet with consumer resistance since consumers must pay all cost per unit over the limit. Thus, prices cannot rise without limit and all forms of indemnity insurance are compatible with market pricing and resource allocation.

Now, let us examine more precisely the impact of indemnity insurance on demand, price, and quantity consumed. As with service benefits, indemnity insurance increases the demand for medical care but in a somewhat different manner. Because of the importance and complexity of this point, Appendixes B and C are devoted to graphical and mathematical expositions to supplement the following verbal discussion.

Consider the situation moments after service benefit or indemnity insurance has been imposed. Let us assume that the large demand increase forces an immediate rise in the total price (insurance payment plus out-of-pocket expense) to the highest level possible at the previous output. In the next instant providers will begin to respond by raising output. But this expansion lowers the out-of-pocket price consumers are willing to pay. The question is, how far will providers expand output for the two types of insurance? Consider what happens to the insurance subsidy (and thus total price received by suppliers) as output increases in each case. For both types of insurance, as output expands, the amount the consumer is willing to pay out of pocket declines by the same amount. Under coinsured service benefits, the insurance payment is simply proportional to the consumer payment. Thus, the insurance subsidy also declines in dollar amount as output increases. The price received by the provider declines relatively rapidly with expansions of output.

On the other hand, if the insurance is of the indemnity type, the subsidy is a constant dollar amount per unit of service. As the output expands the insurance subsidy does not decline in dollar amount. So, total price declines less rapidly with output increases. Therefore, the penalty in the form of lower prices to suppliers for expanding output is lower for indemnity insurance and output, as a result, will increase more and (as we show in Appendixes B and C) price will decline more under indemnity insurance. This kind of insurance leads to lower prices for a given quantity or a greater quantity for a given price (and given insurance payment). This result depends on the partly monopolistic nature of health care supply. Perfectly competitive suppliers would respond identically to the two types of insurance.[18]

To sum up the results of our basic analysis, indemnity benefits result in lower total prices than service benefits for the same consumer out-of-pocket expense and the same quantity consumed. The difference is due to imperfect competition. Under indemnity insurance, the monopoly gains of sellers are lower. Especially for hospitals, less monopoly gain means less wasteful spending.

The Costliness of Care. The incentives resulting from indemnity insurance for choice of the costliness of care are much different from coinsurance. Under indemnity insurance, as long as the payment limit is not set above the price of basic care, additional expenditures or preferred care that is more expensive must be paid entirely out of the consumer's pocket. For example, suppose that a patient is faced with a choice of two hospitals. One is a good quality hospital costing $105 per day, while the second has many rarely used and expensive services and costs $135 per day. If the indemnity insurance pays $100 per day, the consumer must pay directly out of pocket for the higher cost hospital if he favors it. Coinsurance, as we have seen, subsidizes the consumption of more costly care, even if it is only slightly preferred by the consumers; the consumer would pay only a small part of the additional cost of the favored but more expensive hospital. The consumer with indemnity is the more likely to choose less expensive care.

Recent research on the hospital industry by Martin Feldstein has demonstrated how health insurance induces higher cost hospital care as well as increased use of it.[19] Therefore, providing better consumer incentives to carefully consider the additional costs of more expensive

---

[18] This important result is proven mathematically and illustrated graphically in Appendixes B and C.

[19] Martin S. Feldstein, "Quality Change and the Demand for Hospital Care," *Econometrica*, forthcoming.

care is probably the most important advantage of indemnity insurance. These improved incentives would lead to important cost savings if the indemnity were set low enough.

Effects of Indemnity Insurance on Search and Concern for Costs. These advantages of indemnity insurance are amplified given the situation of imperfect competition in the industry. As has been shown, service benefits substantially reduce the incentives for consumer search and information gathering and for cost consciousness. Indemnity insurance, on the other hand, leaves the incentives substantially unaltered as long as the payments allowed by the insurer are less than the price of the services the consumer would choose in the absence of insurance. Since indemnity benefits would probably be set below average prices, any actual indemnity plan would not reduce search incentives by much. The reason for this spur to search and information gathering is that the consumer is allowed to keep the money that he saves by using a lower cost provider, as long as the indemnity amount is less than the lower price. Thus, indemnity insurance does not cause an increase in the monopoly power of individual suppliers owing to lack of consumer knowledge and incentive as do service benefits. Under indemnity, consumers become more aware of alternative suppliers and more willing to switch in response to price differences.

It is useful to note that consumer incentives to search for and use information can be preserved using indemnity insurance even when the coverage is fairly complete. Thus, an efficient market—one with good incentives for consumers to become informed and without the subsidy for overly costly treatment—can exist even with fairly complete insurance if it is of the indemnity type.[20]

Service Mix. Indemnity insurance will affect the service mix since it will alter consumer demand for various services. The effect depends on how the indemnity limits are set for the various services. Indemnity payment limits can be set to give virtually any service mix. The same flexibility exists for service benefits, in that they can produce various service mixes by alteration of coinsurance percentages. However, in the case of indemnity insurance, it is necessary that different limits be set for different services, while it is not necessary that dif-

---

[20] These and related points are made in Mark V. Pauly, "Indemnity Insurance for Health Services Efficiency," *Economics and Business Bulletin*, vol. 23, no. 3 (Fall 1971), pp. 53–59, and in Joseph P. Newhouse and Vincent P. Taylor, "The Subsidy Problem in Hospital Insurance: A Proposal," *Journal of Business*, vol. 43, no. 3 (October 1970), pp. 452–457. The type of insurance Newhouse and Taylor propose is a form of indemnity insurance as it is defined here.

ferent percentages be set for coinsured service benefits (and most actual policies have a flat coinsurance rate). Unfortunately, the information required to hit upon the optimal service mix by adjusting benefit levels is very great, so that only a rough approximation is possible in any case.

It is worth noting that a relative-value fee scale based on relative costs of various services would not lead to an optimal service mix. This is due to the monopoly power of sellers: they expand output more as a result of insurance where quantity consumed is very responsive to price. However, a cost-based scale might produce the best results among feasible scales. The necessary information on demand for specific medical services might simply be too costly to obtain. And, the closer the market approximates a competitive one, the better a cost-based scale would perform.

An issue related to service mix is the problem of redefining services into categories with higher indemnity payments. Providers have an incentive to mislabel what services are performed into higher price categories, for example, by labeling routine office visits as complete physical examinations.

On the surface, this problem appears to affect indemnity benefits more than service benefits, since only in the former are services explicitly defined. But upon thorough consideration, it turns out that this is not the case. Providers could also gain by redefining services paid for by coinsured service benefits into more expensive categories. Two factors would work against such redefinition with either type of benefits. Consumers might question charges as their copayment would increase. Under service benefits, consumers would be faced with a fixed proportion, for example, 20 percent of the extra charge. With an indemnity system, since indemnity payments are often set to achieve a similar degree of cost sharing for the *average* patient, copayment would increase in a similar manner. Of course, the provider could eliminate the consumer's opposition to cheating by not bothering to collect the copayment. This could occur under either type of benefit. The other inhibiting factor is claims review by the insurer, but this is also applicable to either type of benefit. Indeed, there is a great deal of accumulated experience with claims review under both types of benefits in private insurance companies (both Blue Cross–Blue Shield plans and commercial insurers). Thus, problems in defining medical services should not be a factor in favoring one type of insurance benefit over the other.

A Disadvantage of Indemnity Insurance and Possible Modifications. The advantages of indemnity insurance in general and especially for

NHI are very important. They include lower prices, more competitive and efficient markets, more cost-conscious consumers, and better incentives to avoid overuse of the very costly forms of medical care. However, indemnity insurance is not without its problems.

A disadvantage is that consumers would face more risk under an indemnity plan. For example, suppose that the plan provided a certain dollar amount per surgical procedure. There is a possibility that in spite of the incentives built in, the consumer might find himself a very expensive physician. In such a situation, the amount of out-of-pocket expense might be large.

If this risk problem were to be a serious deterrent to the adoption of an indemnity plan, indemnity insurance could be combined with coinsurance in a manner suggested by Pauly.[21] The insurer could pay part of the expenses above the dollar limit, that is, expenses exceeding the dollar limit could be covered by a coinsurance policy. Further, there could be a deductible so that only if expenses exceeded the insurance payments by a great deal would the coinsurance begin. This is how commercial indemnity insurance handles hospital ancillary services. These services do not have specific dollar limits associated with them, but expenses are covered with service benefits, usually with a coinsurance feature.

Another way to reduce the risk of indemnity insurance is to provide a major medical insurance plan which takes over, with some coinsurance rate, if the consumer incurs sufficient out-of-pocket expense under the indemnity plan to exceed a deductible. Some current commercial insurance policies with an indemnity basic plan and major medical insurance provide exactly such coverage. Such plans reduce the total financial risk of the consumer while preserving the superior incentives of indemnity insurance for most illness episodes and thus most medical care.

Impacts of Deductibles

A supplement to coinsurance and indemnity benefits as ways of inducing consumers to consider cost is the deductible, that is, a requirement that the consumer pay the first costs incurred during a certain span of time (often one year). These provisions are common in many health and other types of insurance plans (auto collision, fire). Since the impact of deductibles is similar for both indemnity and service benefit insurance, we will discuss it in the context of service benefits only. Essentially the same arguments apply to deductible provisions of in-

---

[21] Pauly, "Indemnity Insurance," pp. 57–58.

demnity insurance, except that the incentives to search are strong in any case and are not affected by the addition of the deductible.

Even restricting ourselves to the deductible provisions of service benefits schemes, there are three cases to consider. The first case, where the consumer is virtually certain not to exceed the deductible, is quite simple. The consumer behaves as if he had no insurance. Thus, his demand for medical care will not be increased by the insurance. He will bear the true costs of higher quality care and more expensive services, so that his choices will be efficient. The second case is that of the consumer who is virtually certain to exceed the deductible. Many consumers are currently in this position if they have insurance plans with small deductibles (say $100 per family per year). Again, analysis of this consumer's case is simple. The deductible feature will not affect the consumer at all. He will behave precisely as if the insurance had no deductible and covered all his expenses in the same manner (with the same coinsurance rate). The deductible may save administrative costs, but it will not reduce demand for medical care in this case, nor induce search, weighing of costs in a rational way, or other such behavior.

The more interesting and more important case is that of the consumer who is uncertain whether he will exceed the deductible. In this intermediate range, the consumer will demand less than he would if he had the policy with no deductible, because the expected payment out of pocket is greater with a deductible. For example, if the consumer had a policy with complete coverage and a deductible, his expected payment would be some proportion of costs. Therefore, he would demand health care as if he had a policy with some coinsurance. Clearly, the larger the deductible, the larger the coinsurance rate that would induce the same behavior. Matters are further complicated by the fact that the same person may move from the uncertain category to the category where he is certain to exceed or not exceed the deductible over the period for which the deductible is defined. Nonetheless, the overall market impact of deductibles is much like coinsurance, since the market responds to average consumer behavior.[22]

If we turn to the effect of deductibles on consumer search and concern for costs, matters get more complicated. Many observers believe that the scope and impact of consumer incentives is larger for smaller medical expenditures, which are more likely to be elective. If this is the case, deductibles will have a stronger positive impact on

---

[22] For an analysis of the theory of deductibles and consumer behavior, see Emmett B. Keeler, Joseph P. Newhouse, and Charles E. Phelps, "Deductibles and Demand for Medical Services: The Theory of a Consumer Facing a Variable Price Schedule under Uncertainty," *Econometrica*, forthcoming.

consumer behavior and thus weaken the monopoly position of providers more than equivalent (in terms of expected consumer out-of-pocket expenses) coinsurance. Deductibles increase the incentive for search and cost consciousness for small expenses and decrease the incentives for larger expenses. An argument of this sort lies behind Feldstein's proposal for NHI with very large (perhaps 10 percent of family income) deductibles.[23]

A problem with consumer copayment provisions and especially large deductibles is that consumers may buy private insurance to fill in the out-of-pocket payments. Such extra insurance frustrates the cost control goals of the copayment provisions. Further, consumers who purchased this insurance would demand more benefits from the government plan as well since the supplementary insurance would raise their demand for health care in general. Empirical research by Keeler, Morrow, and Newhouse indicate that demand for supplemental insurance would be small, unless the current tax subsidy for health insurance were retained.[24] In any case, demand for such insurance could be easily reduced by a small tax.

---

[23] See Martin Feldstein, "A New Approach to National Health Insurance," *Public Interest*, no. 23 (Spring 1971).

[24] Emmett Keeler, Daniel T. Morrow, and Joseph P. Newhouse, "The Demand for Supplementary Health Insurance, or Do Deductibles Matter?" *Journal of Political Economy*, vol. 85, no. 4 (August 1977), pp. 799–800.

4

Fee and Price Regulation under Public Insurance

At present, many Americans have private health insurance coverage that pays the entire cost of some medical procedures. In terms of economic efficiency, this is too much insurance. This is to say that if these consumers were confronted with the true costs of such complete insurance, they would choose somewhat incomplete insurance, at a savings in premiums. People choose such full coverage not because they are irrational, but because of the existing tax subsidies favoring health insurance and the regulatory advantages of the Blue Cross and Blue Shield insurers which are committed to that type of insurance.[1]

Since full coverage insurance is now fairly common, it may be politically expedient for a national health insurance plan to provide full coverage despite its problems. However, as shown above, full coverage service benefits are incompatible with the use of the market to allocate or assist in the allocation of medical resources. Further, as average benefits approach full coverage and/or the number of consumers with full coverage becomes high, the power of the medical market to discipline inefficiency and induce cost consciousness and search behavior

---

[1] See Martin Feldstein, "The Welfare Loss of Excess Health Insurance," *Journal of Political Economy*, vol. 81, no. 2 (March-April 1973); Martin S. Feldstein and Elizabeth Allison, "Tax Subsidies of Private Health Insurance: Distribution, Revenue Loss and Effects," in *The Economics of Federal Subsidy Programs* (Washington, D.C.: U.S. Congress, Joint Economic Committee, 1974); and Bridger Mitchell and Ronald Vogel, "Health and Taxes: An Assessment of the Medical Deduction," *Southern Economic Journal*, vol. 41 (April 1975), for discussion of the excessiveness of existing health insurance and the tax subsidies that influence it. Mark V. Pauly shows a type of high information cost to be the basis of overinsurance in "Overinsurance and the Public Provision of Insurance: The Roles of Moral Hazard and Adverse Selection," *Quarterly Journal of Economics*, vol. 88, no. 1 (February 1974), pp. 44–62. The role of regulatory advantages for Blue Cross and Blue Shield insurers is the focus of H. E. Frech III, "The Regulation of Health Insurance," Ph.D. diss., University of California, Los Angeles, 1974. This paper also includes a proof that in the presence of moral hazard, incomplete insurance is optimal, pp. 19–35.

may become very weak. If so, the costs of medical care might increase rapidly, even if the fully explosive case of full coverage for everyone is not reached. Whether the medical care market is destroyed or only weakened by overly complete NHI, it is unlikely that the designers of the system would allow prices and costs to rise almost without limit. The political pressure for regulation is very strong.

Many current NHI proposals include price controls (for example, the Kennedy-Corman, Mills, Schenebeli, Packwood, Kennedy-Mills, and Ullman bills).[2] Further, there is considerable movement toward price controls at present, even without the imposition of NHI.[3] The Medicare and Medicaid plans include physician reimbursement ceilings, and the Carter administration has proposed hospital price controls in HR 6575 (see above, chapter 2). In what follows, we examine price regulation with special emphasis on efforts to base regulatory prices on market ones. It turns out that if the regulation covers all consumers, borrowing market prices produces strong inflationary pressures.

Fee Schedules: Administratively Set Price Controls

An alternative to consider is simple price regulation which includes two distinguishable cases. The first is where the price set by a government agency is the ceiling price—additional charges directly to the consumer by the providers of care are prohibited. This is a common type of regulation and is often called "mandatory assignment" in the context of current government programs. Currently, most Medicaid programs reimburse physicians and other professionals in this manner. The second possibility is that providers be allowed to charge the patient something extra, in effect, the difference between the price and the regulated fee. This is the method used by CHAMPUS, the government program for military personnel who use civilian facilities, and in Medicare, where participating physicians may choose for each patient whether to accept assignment or to charge more than the Medicare fee.

Fee Schedules with Extra Charges Prohibited. In exploring fee schedules, we deal first with standardized units of medical care and then con-

---

[2] Thomas D. Hall, "Proposals under Consideration," in Cotton M. Lindsay, ed., *New Directions in Public Health Care* (San Francisco: Institute for Contemporary Studies, 1976), pp. 167–208.

[3] See William Dowling, "Prospective Rate Setting: Concept and Practice," *Topics in Health Care Financing*, vol. 3, no. 2 (Winter 1976), pp. 7–37, for a discussion of the current status of hospital price regulation. Paul B. Ginsburg, "Regulating the Price of Hospital Care," in Thomas G. Moore, ed., *Regulatory Reform* (Washington, D.C.: American Enterprise Institute, forthcoming).

sider the problem of different fees for different services. For simplicity, we examine the case of the Ontario provincial health insurance program—where consumers have full coverage service benefit insurance. Many favor this type of plan because it limits physician incomes. For consumers, medical care has a zero money price: they will demand it to the point where an additional unit of care has no value to them. Providers, on the other hand, react to a different price (the regulatory ceiling price). In this situation, providers will furnish services up to the point where their marginal cost is equal to the regulated price. There is no reason to expect the decisions of providers and consumers to mesh in this situation because price is not allowed to equate supply with demand. Thus, if the regulation actually reduces prices, consumers will demand more care than suppliers choose to provide, and, if fees are somehow set very high, vice versa.[4] Such a phenomenon is frequently observed in the Medicaid program, where many physicians refuse to serve Medicaid patients. Since it is more likely fees would be low and that the quantity demanded would exceed the quantity supplied, we will consider that case.

In the situation of demand in excess of supply, nonprice rationing is necessary: providers must somehow decide which consumers to serve. One can hope that the rationing might be accomplished at least partly on the basis of the medical importance of the care. If so, relatively serious conditions where medical care could help would be treated while less severe cases and those where medical care could contribute little would be left untreated. But even perfect professional rationing has disadvantages, and, unfortunately, other considerations can be expected to enter into the rationing decision. Providers are likely to deliver care to patients whom they find more attractive personally or scientifically—friends, patients with pleasing, attractive personalities and intriguing medical complaints.[5] Commonly, physicians refuse to accept new patients while all demands of existing patients are served.

---

[4] This discussion has assumed that providers will offer more services when fees are higher. It should be noted that some observers suggest that for *physicians*, hours of work may decline when fees increase (Uwe Reinhardt, *Physician Productivity and the Demand for Health Manpower* [Cambridge, Mass.: Ballinger, 1975]). This may or may not cause *services* to decline. Empirical evidence in Frank A. Sloan, "A Microanalysis of Physicians' Hours of Work Decisions," in Mark Perlman, ed., *Economics of Health and Medical Care* (London: Halsted, 1974), pp. 302–325, shows no significant impact of fees on hours of work. Such results do not detract from the notion that quantities of services produced would equal the quantities demanded only by coincidence.

[5] See Martin S. Feldstein, "The Rising Price of Physician Services," *Review of Economics and Statistics*, vol. 52, no. 2 (May 1970), pp. 121–133, for a discussion of the importance of physician preferences for interesting medical cases.

In a system so regulated, suppliers have no incentive to ration medical care in accordance with consumer preferences.[6]

Professional Nonprice Rationing and Consumer Welfare. Excess demand leaves providers without market incentives, a situation with some surprising and serious implications. First, providers would be able to locate in areas they find pleasant with no income sacrifice. Thus, such unpleasant areas as inner cities and some rural areas would have less attraction than under a market system and would lose providers to the more pleasant suburbs and to professionally interesting medical centers. Ongoing research by Rod D. Fraser indicates that the national health care schemes in several developed countries, including Canada and Japan, have led to physician migration to urban areas.[7] On the other hand, if the market system were allowed to work, less attractive areas could attract physicians with a combination of higher fees and opportunity for higher incomes by providing more services.

Interestingly, the same impact would be felt in terms of specialty choice. A situation of general excess demand would lead physicians to choose specialties that are considered more interesting and/or more pleasant, at the expense of less interesting or less attractive specialties. One of the victims of this is likely to be general or family practice, a field many feel is undermanned as it is.

Thus, complete insurance and binding price regulation would lead to subtle incentives for geographic and specialty choices that suit physicians but are unlikely to correspond to consumer preferences. This type of insurance and regulation eliminates the ways consumer preferences can influence physician choices. The same effect would be felt by hospitals for choice of location and service mix. These influences are so subtle that it is unlikely that physicians and hospitals would recognize their existence. The nonprice rationing problem is both more subtle and more serious than one might imagine, especially in the long run.

Consumers' Information Advantages. Even if physicians were to become perfectly altruistic and try to allocate resources in accordance with consumer preferences, they are at a more serious informational

---

[6] Physicians making similar decisions in competing health maintenance organizations (HMOs) have far better incentives to take account of consumer preferences. See the analysis of HMOs below.

[7] Private conversation with Rod D. Fraser, Queen's University, Kingston, Ontario, June 14, 1977. For more on this general topic, see H. E. Frech III, "The Case of the Medical Care Industry," in Thomas G. Moore, ed., *Regulatory Reform* (Washington, D.C.: American Enterprise Institute, forthcoming).

disadvantage when prices are controlled. Much of the benefit of medical care is subjective: alleviation of loneliness, symptomatic relief, reassurance, comfort, and so on. The subjective nature of the benefits of much medical care is the reason that even the fairly large variations in health care use observed in the United States have virtually no impact on such objective measures of health as life expectancy and disability.[8] Physicians are at an obvious disadvantage in evaluating the subjective benefits of medical care. Allocations based on medical severity (perhaps defined as the danger to life) are not likely to mirror consumer preferences very well, considering that a very small proportion of medical care is rendered in life-threatening cases.

For example, consider a patient in some pain, which can be alleviated by a risky operation. The appropriate values to place on both the pain and the risk are entirely subjective: they depend strictly on the values of the patient. No amount of medical information concerning the probabilities of various outcomes can decide the issue. A great deal of medical care involves such grey areas as subjective suffering and/or feelings about risk. For such cases, nonprice rationing, even by a perfectly altruistic professional, is likely to be very inaccurate in matching what an informed consumer facing true costs would prefer.

Since professional incentives differ from those of consumers and professionals are at an important informational disadvantage for many medical decisions, the nonprice rationing made necessary by prohibition of consumer payments above a regulated price would be very imperfect and would lead to considerable waste.

The government may respond with direct regulation, attempting to make the rationing process approximate consumer preferences more closely. But this would be terribly difficult, considering the informational disadvantage of the government and the fact that regulated prices convey no information about consumer satisfaction.

Serious as these problems are, an even worse problem with prohibiting extra payments to providers may be the maintenance of quality. With excess demand for their services, providers would have an incentive to cut quality and amenities to the lowest level consistent

---

[8] For recent research on the small impact of health care on health, see Lee Benham and Alexandra Benham, "The Impact of Incremental Medical Services on Health Status, 1964–1970," in Ronald Andersen, Joanna Kravits, and Odin Anderson, eds., *Equity in Health Services: Empirical Analysis in Social Policy* (Cambridge, Mass.: Ballinger, 1975), pp. 217–227. For an excellent analysis of perinatal mortality, the one area where medical care does seem to have a large impact, see Ronald L. Williams, "Explaining a Health Care Paradox," *Policy Sciences*, vol. 6 (1975), pp. 91–101, and "Outcome-Based Measurements of Medical Care Output: The Case of Maternal and Infant Health," Ph.D. dissertation, University of California, Santa Barbara, 1974.

with malpractice law.[9] For example, waiting times would lengthen, less time would be spent with patients for each procedure, and so on.

The only incentive for the maintenance of quality and attractiveness above the bare minimum is the desire of the provider to be able to choose the people he prefers to serve. Here the competition of suppliers for the right to discriminate among consumers may be an important aid in the maintenance of quality. Unfortunately, this sort of competition benefits only those whom the providers prefer to serve and is not likely to benefit the poor or members of unpopular minorities.

Of course, devotion to professional standards of conduct will be a force tending to support quality levels in the absence of specific incentives for quality. However, professional standards are unlikely to have any effect beyond narrowly defined quality, and, at least with some providers, amenities important to consumers will decline. In any case, the only forces preventing the quality level from plummeting are the desire to maintain a large pool of cases from which to choose the most attractive or interesting, malpractice law, and devotion to professional standards. In such a situation, a large degree of detailed government quality regulation may be valuable, even with all the bureaucratic problems that it entails.[10]

Sadly, the technology needed for such regulation is lacking. Observers do not agree on basic definitions of medical quality, much less on how to regulate it. As a result, existing quality regulation pertains to the inputs into the medical process, not the actual quality of the care provided. Current input regulation takes two forms: first, extensive licensure of medical practitioners and technicians of all sorts with requirements for minimum levels of educational background, and second, for institutions, regulation of levels and types of staffing and other inputs—and both forms have been criticized for inefficiency.[11] Professional standards review organizations are attempting to use process measures of quality regulation (review of medical records), but it will be some time before the cost-effectiveness of this approach can be assessed. There is concern at present that the process will be expensive but sensitive enough to detect only gross incompetence.[12] NHI with full coverage and price regulation where providers are not allowed to

---

[9] Lawrence J. White, "Quality Variation When Prices Are Regulated," *Bell Journal of Economics and Management Science*, vol. 3, no. 2 (Autumn 1972), pp. 425–436.

[10] Clark C. Havighurst and James Blumstein, "Coping with Quality/Cost Trade-Offs in Medical Care: The Role of PSROs," *Northwestern University Law Review*, vol. 70, no. 6 (March-April 1975), pp. 62–66.

[11] H. E. Frech III, "Occupational Licensure and Health Care Productivity," in John A. Rafferty, ed., *Health Manpower and Productivity* (Lexington, Mass.: Heath, 1975), pp. 119–139, and Frech, "Regulatory Reform."

[12] Havighurst and Blumstein, "Coping with Quality/Cost Trade-Offs," pp. 62–68.

charge more than the regulated fee would put a great deal of reliance on these regulatory measures, which are widely believed to be both ineffective and wasteful in the current situation.

To avoid the difficult problems of rationing, of unfortunate geographic, specialty, and service mix choices, and of quality maintenance, policy makers may allow some appropriate incentives to work to avoid excess demand. In a regulatory context, these goals can be achieved by allowing providers to charge consumers an out-of-pocket amount above the regulated fee. This situation therefore deserves our attention.

Fee Schedules with Extra Charges Allowed. Price regulation where providers are allowed to charge consumers more than the regulated amount is precisely equivalent to indemnity insurance. The provider gets the regulated amount from the insurer (in the full coverage insurance case we are considering), while the consumer pays out of pocket the remainder (if any) of the bill. This is identical to the situation that would obtain if the insurer simply provided indemnity insurance with the benefits equal to the regulated price. Further, the development of the fee schedule is the same exercise as the setting of levels of insurance payment in indemnity insurance.

If such regulations are imposed upon a system with coinsurance it again is equivalent to indemnity insurance, but with a benefit payment equal to the proportion paid by the insurer multiplied by the regulated price. For example, if the regulated price for a service were $200 and the coinsurance rate were 80 percent, the resulting price, quantity, and so on would be identical to the case where the consumers held indemnity insurance that paid $160 for the service. This is the situation for a substantial proportion of Medicare physician care cases. Thus, one can get to a situation of indemnity insurance in more than one way.

The Problem of Setting Regulated Fees. The problem of determining regulated prices is a truly massive one. One cannot simply look at the market and use those prices. When all are insured, initial market prices become increasingly obsolete over time—leading to increasing distortions. Market prices can be used over the long haul only if NHI applies to only a part of the total medical care market. In this case, the prices observed in the uncontrolled or free market sector could be taken as rough guides to the correct prices, because they would roughly equal the costs of providing the services. Further, the regulated prices could not be very much less than the market sector prices, for the obvious reason that consumers under the government program would not be able to obtain care if the prices were set too much below what providers could get in the market sector. Thus, the government's ability to limit costs by regulation is limited.

The prices from the market sector would be only approximate guides for regulation because they are influenced by a certain amount of monopoly power on the part of the providers: the prices across services and the level of services would reflect the profit-maximizing conditions for a monopolist. These would be systematically too high, and, in addition, the relative prices would reflect differences in price sensitivities for individual services, as well as differences in costs. But, rough as they are, these market prices would be virtually the only possible guides to regulatory pricing. The reasons for this are the great complexity of medical care and the fact that much of the input is in the form of physician time at various tasks, which make cost-based regulation essentially arbitrary. The valuation of the physician time input is necessarily a highly subjective affair. Existing fee schedules and relative-value scales which were constructed by providers are essentially market-based, although the schedules were apparently designed with an eye to increasing provider incomes by raising prices for services which are not very price-sensitive.[13]

Of course, there is a problem in determining what the market prices actually are. For each service, there would be a large range of prices, corresponding to divergences in quality, locality, amenities, costs of practice, differences in resources, and so on. Thus, even a market-based scheme would face some difficult initial problems.

The overall character of a public program that includes only part of the population can be influenced by the choice of how to interpret the idea of market-based fees. This is true of all dimensions of health care, but perhaps most obvious for access. If fees are set in accordance with an interpretation of the market price that corresponds to basic care, many providers who provide relatively more attractive and costly care would not participate, unless they were allowed to charge patients more than the fee set by the regulation. Lower fees would lead to more difficult access and lower quality for the covered population. Fear of the access problem explains why the current Medicare program allows extra out-of-pocket charges. Fees that are too high will lead to consumption of excessive amounts of care that are too high in quality and amenities, as suppliers compete for members of the covered population by nonprice means.

If the NHI scheme is universal, setting prices becomes much more difficult. In this case, there would be no market to generate prices for

---

[13] H. E. Frech III, "Expanding the FTC Health Care Program," *Federal Trade Commission Program Budget Mid-Year Review*, vol. 3 (1976), pp. CA-37–CA-64.

the regulatory officials to use as guides. In such a difficult situation, the best solution may be to use the advice of the medical suppliers themselves. Even though they have a direct financial stake in the outcome, they have reasonable intuition on the matter of relative costs of alternative services. Further, the regulatory officials might be able to determine if there is substantial monopolistic exploitation in the prices chosen by suppliers. This is possible only if the insurance is less than complete or if additional payments are allowed over the regulated price. For only in this situation can one observe market demand.

"Usual, Customary, and Prevailing" Limits to Prices

Determining a schedule of fees or prices is clearly very difficult. Because of these problems, regulators may be tempted to allow information taken from the market to set and update prices. They and insurers have turned to limiting fees to those that are "usual, customary, and prevailing," rather than to specific fee schedules. The "usual and customary" provisions reduce the ability of the provider to discriminate against insured patients by charging them higher prices (as would be rational); cost-based reimbursement for hospitals performs the same function even more effectively. Here, insured customers cannot be charged more than costs, thus limiting discrimination against them and their insurer.

The last provision prevents the provider from charging more than prevailing prices. These prices are obtained by surveying actual rates and selecting a percentile in the distribution of rates for each service (usually between the seventy-fifth percentile for Medicare and the ninetieth percentile for some Blue Shield plans). The "usual and customary" provisions are very difficult to enforce because of the complexity of medical markets, the potential for adjustment of the prices to nonmembers of the insurance plan to maximize profit over both markets, and the opportunity to claim charity as a basis for providing care at a lower price for those not covered by the plan. With a universal NHI plan, the "usual and customary" provisions would have no meaning, unless deductibles were very large so that some care was effectively uninsured.

Once the level of fees is determined by survey, this type of regulation is identical to a fee schedule. The only differences are that prices can vary by physician and by area and that the regulator's discretion regarding changes in prices is surrendered to an automatic mechanism, related to actual pricing. The results of this automatic mechanism over time can be predicted. Where insurance coverage is universal and complete, it leads to continual price inflation. (The analysis is similar but more complex under universal coinsurance.) To see this, think of the reaction of providers when a new, higher regulatory rate is announced. Clearly, they raise their prices. But, as providers raise their prices, the average price will rise and, more important, whatever percentile is chosen for determining the price controls will rise.

Thus, at the next time to adjust the price, the prevailing rate will be found to be higher, so that the regulated rate must be set higher. And the process will repeat itself until prices are so high and the quantity supplied so great that consumers are saturated with medical care—they place no value on an additional unit.[14] The rate of inflation depends solely on the percentile chosen and on how often the schedule is revised. This inflationary result may be what the late Senator Clinton Anderson envisioned when he said: "I am concerned that the concept of "usual, customary, and prevailing" has provided a floor rather than a ceiling and that every year since these programs began, the "usual" has become the unusual and the "prevailing" has not prevailed."[15] Fundamentally, this method of setting fees makes sense only if the sector with regulated insurance is small relative to the market as a whole. If so, the method becomes a convenient way of borrowing market prices for use in the regulations. If the insured regulated sector is large, however, the method has its own inflationary dynamics (to the point of consumer satiation with medical care) because there is no independent market sector from which to borrow prices.

As a result of experiencing the physician fee inflation predicted by our analysis, Medicare has recently changed to a policy where the inflation in the fee level is limited by an economic index of the costs of inputs into physician services. This policy does reduce the pressure for inflation, but does not eliminate it. Some problems remain, particularly over a span of time.

First, the input prices considered in formulating the economic index include a service industry wage index to measure changes in value of the physician's time. The appropriateness of such a proxy depends on the correlation—unlikely to be very high—between changes in the value of physician time and changes in service industry wages. Second, the index takes no account of technical change. If some new techniques are developed that allow the physicians to produce services using fewer inputs, the economic index is not reduced, since it is based only on input prices. As technical change proceeds over time, the index would become less accurate.

---

[14] The result that the price inflation will stop only when consumer demand is saturated is proven mathematically in Appendix C.

[15] U.S. Congress, Senate, Committee on Finance, *Medicare and Medicaid: Hearings, Part I,* 91st Congress, 2nd session, 1970, p. 5.

In conclusion, there is no easy way out of the problems of setting prices if the market mechanism is completely eliminated. There is no simple mechanical device that can set these prices without creating immense problems of its own and leading to arbitrary, incorrect prices or a great deal of price inflation or both. As dangerous as it is, the intuition of financially interested parties (the providers) is likely to be the only feasible guide in the long run if the market mechanism is abandoned.

5

Public Insurance through Health Maintenance Organizations

During the 1930s the prepaid group practice, an innovation in the organization of medical care in the United States, was developed. Organizations of physicians practicing together offered reasonably comprehensive medical care to subscribers for a fixed annual fee. Despite extensive opposition from the AMA,[1] a number of prepaid group practices grew rapidly and developed national reputations.[2]

In 1970 the Nixon administration decided to encourage the growth of such practices as part of a policy of dealing with health care problems through the private sector. The term "health maintenance organization" (HMO) was coined to describe organizations that delivered comprehensive medical services to enrolled populations on a capitation basis.[3] Encompassed by the definition are both prepaid group practices and organizations such as medical societies offering prepaid services through associated solo practitioners with central claims review designed to cut utilization. The latter is often referred to as the medical foundation model or as an independent practice association.

---

[1] See Reuben A. Kessel, "The AMA and the Supply of Physicians," *Law and Contemporary Problems*, vol. 38 (Autumn 1970), pp. 267–283; and David Barton, "Alternative Institutional Arrangements for Medical Care Insurance," (Ph.D. dissertation, University of Virginia, 1974), pp. 74–141, for descriptions of the astounding campaign against prepaid group practices.

[2] Among the notable are: Kaiser-Permanente, Group Health Cooperative of Puget Sound (state of Washington), Group Health Association of Washington, D.C., and Health Insurance Plan of Greater New York.

[3] Paul M. Ellwood, "Restructuring the Health Delivery System: Will the Health Maintenance Strategy Work?" in *Health Maintenance Organizations: A Reconfiguration of the Health Services System, Proceedings of the Thirteenth Annual Symposium on Hospital Affairs* (Chicago: Center for Health Administration Studies, 1971), pp. 2–11.

Standard Analysis of HMO Incentives

The literature on HMOs emphasizes that since they earn a fixed annual fee for medical services, their financial incentive is to reduce utilization.[4] In contrast, fee-for-service providers tend to increase their income as utilization increases. HMO patients, on the other hand, have incentives to use more services, since they do not face the deductibles commonly encountered in traditional insurance policies.

Another incentive in HMOs is to use preventive care up to the point where the effectiveness of an additional unit in avoiding future medical expense is equal to its cost. However, in spite of the conventional wisdom, it is not clear whether this means that HMOs deliver more preventive care than do fee-for-service providers. There is empirical evidence that they do not;[5] cost-effective preventive care may already be generally provided to most consumers who are not indigent. There is an incentive for fee-for-service providers to recommend preventive care simply because it is profitable to deliver, and, since it is a small, predictable expense, consumers may be responsive to the advice.

A number of additional alleged incentives of HMOs are based on confusing prepayment with other variations in health delivery. Some allege that HMOs have an incentive to use more ancillary (nonphysician) personnel, but fee-for-service group practices have the same incentives and advantages in manpower substitution: both would try to produce efficiently. Others allege that HMOs substitute ambulatory care for inpatient care, but that is really an incentive for all patients whose insurance covers both types of care equally well.

Few innovations are without disadvantages, and the HMO is no exception. Just as the incentive to "overdoctor" is eliminated, one to "underdoctor" is established. Higher service needs by patients in the future will only partially dissuade underdoctoring because people are

---

[4] See, for example, the discussion of health maintenance organizations in Avedis Donabedian, "An Evaluation of Prepaid Group Practice," *Inquiry*, vol. 6 (September 1969), pp. 3–27, and Milton Roemer and William Shonick, "HMO Performance: The Recent Evidence," *Milbank Memorial Fund Quarterly: Health and Society*, vol. 51 (Summer 1973), pp. 271–317.

There are skeptics. Klarman contends that HMO utilization reductions are caused by limited access to hospitals rather than prepayment. See Herbert E. Klarman, "Analysis of the HMO Proposal: Its Assumptions, Implications and Prospects," in *Health Maintenance Organizations*, pp. 24–33, and "Major Public Initiatives in Health Care," *The Public Interest*, vol. 34, no. 1 (Winter 1974), pp. 106–122. However, limited access to hospitals may be designed into HMOs in order to limit utilization.

[5] Clifton Gaus, Barbara Cooper, and Constance Hirschman, "Contrasts in HMO and Fee-for-Service Performance," *Social Security Bulletin*, vol. 39 (May 1976), pp. 3–14.

mobile and might not be enrolled in the future, and because the effect of underdoctoring is often increased discomfort at present rather than greater service needs in the future. There is also an incentive to reduce amenities and the "caring" function. Competition with other HMOs and with fee-for-service providers is important to limit the underutilization incentives.

The question of HMO incentives is often treated too glibly. Most writers implicitly assume that each physician faces a direct personal financial incentive to control costs. But even in physician-owned prepaid group practices, the individual physician is usually salaried and shares the benefit of reduced utilization with others in the group. Some prepaid group practices are "owned" by consumer groups rather than physicians, further weakening these incentives. In prepaid groups the incentive to overdoctor clearly vanishes, but in the foundation model even this incentive remains. While overdoctoring hurts the foundation, it is profitable for the individual physician since he is actually paid on a fee-for-service basis. Foundations attempt to discourage overdoctoring through claims review.[6] This is similar to administrative cost controls by private insurers, except that the foundation has a local monopoly and is controlled by physicians. Presumably, these features have made foundation cost controls acceptable to physicians and hospitals while insurer cost controls are not.

A private health insurer has incentives to monitor the behavior of the consumers and providers in order to control costs, just as an HMO does. However, the opposition of organized medicine has prevented such controls from achieving very much.[7] One would expect that a competitive medical care system would lead to a continuum of organizations insuring medical care. At one extreme would be the prepaid group practice, with very tight control of medical care provision, and at the other would be the modern type of private health insurer, with almost no controls on costs other than consumer copayment. Most insurers would probably inhabit the region between the extremes, with fairly potent administrative cost controls.

In what follows, we ignore administrative cost controls by private health insurers to concentrate on the more traditional type of HMO.

---

[6] There is evidence that foundation-type HMOs have not been as successful as prepaid group practices in reducing utilization. See Gaus, Cooper, and Hirschman, "Contrasts in HMO and Fee-for-Service Performance."

[7] See Clark C. Havighurst, "Controlling Health Care Costs: Strengthening the Private Sector's Hand," *Journal of Health Politics, Policy and Law*, vol. 1, no. 4 (Winter 1977), and Lawrence Goldberg and Warren Greenberg, "The Effect of Physician-Controlled Health Insurance: U.S. v. Oregon State Medical Society," *Journal of Health Politics, Policy and Law*, vol. 2, no. 1 (Spring 1977).

But this is merely our choice of topic. We believe that administrative cost control as a means of insurer competition is potentially very powerful.

Actual HMO Experience

There is now extensive literature documenting savings in costs and utilization in HMOs, with most research being on the group practice model.[8] A study of California state employees found that families enrolled in the Kaiser-Permanente plan had costs 23 percent lower than those enrolled in a commercial insurance plan.[9] One of the most extensive studies of HMOs, by Hetherington et al., compared two prepaid groups—Kaiser and Ross-Loos—with two Blue Cross plans and two commercial plans. Per capita expenses in the prepaid groups were 29 percent lower than in the commercial plans and 46 percent lower than in Blue Cross. The populations were not matched, but the demographic characteristics indicated that the prepaid groups' members were likely to be the high utilizers.[10] Corbin and Krute studied matched samples of Medicare beneficiaries in a number of prepaid group practices, and found that HMO members' costs were 6 to 34 percent lower than those of non-HMO beneficiaries.[11] This is especially interesting, since Medicare reimbursed the HMOs on a cost basis. However, the Medicare proportion of enrollees in each plan was small, so that the departure from prepayment for this group probably had little effect on overall group behavior.

Cost studies point to reduction in hospital utilization as the major source of cost savings. For example, the Hetherington study compared hospital utilization of federal prepaid group enrollees with federal Blue Cross subscribers in the same state and found a utilization reduction of 35–70 percent.[12] Barton made statistical adjustments for population characteristics and found a 59 percent reduction in hospital use.[13] Reidel et al. compared federal employees enrolled in the Group Health

---

[8] ICF Incorporated, *Selected Use of Competition by Health Systems Agencies,* final report under contract HEW–HRA–230–75–0071 (Washington, D.C., December 1976), chap. III was drawn upon heavily for the following section.

[9] D. Dozier et al., *1970–71 Survey of Consumer Experience Report of the State of California Employees' Medical and Hospital Care Program* (Sacramento: State of California, 1973).

[10] R. Hetherington, C. Hopkins, and M. Roemer, *Health Insurance Plans: Promise and Performance* (New York: Wiley, 1975).

[11] Mildred Corbin and Aaron Krute, "Some Aspects of Medicare Experience with Group Payment Plans," *Social Security Bulletin,* vol. 38 (March 1975), pp. 3–11.

[12] Hetherington, Hopkins, and Roemer, *Health Insurance Plans.*

[13] Barton, "Alternative Institutional Arrangements," pp. 57, 60, 146–149.

Association of Washington, D.C., with a demographically comparable group of federal Blue Cross subscribers and found a 55 percent reduction in hospital utilization.[14] Gaus, Cooper, and Hirschman studied Medicaid recipients and found a 62 percent reduction in hospital use.[15]

Comparable savings are not found in ambulatory care. Some studies show a reduction in ambulatory care use, but others show increases. The ICF, Inc., review of this literature indicates that when utilization increases, it usually means a higher proportion of enrollees using services rather than more visits per utilizer.[16]

The record of other types of HMO is not as good as the prepaid group practices. While controlled comparison studies have not been conducted for foundation-type HMOs, crude comparisons show reductions in utilization compared with Blue Cross plans, but smaller than in prepaid groups. In the Gaus et al. study of Medicaid, no reduction was found,[17] by ICF, Inc., maintains that this is explainable by the absence of financial incentives on physicians for hospital utilization in the particular plans studied. Indeed, ICF, Inc., discusses a foundation-type HMO with no financial risk at all for physicians and no peer review for hospitalization which has hospitalization rates substantially above Blue Cross rates.[18] The plan is no longer functioning.

Identity of Insurer and Provider in HMOs

One of the authors commonly asks his students why standard Blue Cross–Blue Shield service benefit insurance does not constitute an HMO. The benefits are clearly comprehensive, the policyholders constitute an enrolled population, and the insurance premiums are annual. The difference is that Blue Cross–Blue Shield plans do not provide medical care. Their contract with the policyholder calls for them to reimburse providers of care for services, rather than to provide the service themselves. Thus with conventional health insurance, there is specialization between a firm that produces insurance and one that produces medical services. These two types of firms deal with each other through a market, and whatever is saved in fees and utilization of health care accrues to the insurer. In the HMO, on the other hand, the insurer and the pro-

---

[14] D. Reidel et al., *Federal Employees Health Benefits Program-Utilization Study* (Washington, D.C.: U.S. Department of Health, Education, and Welfare, 1975).

[15] Gaus, Cooper, and Hirschman, "Contrasts in HMO and Fee-for-Service Performance."

[16] ICF, Inc., *Selected Use of Competition*, pp. III–11.

[17] Gaus, Cooper, and Hirschman, "Contrasts in HMO and Fee-for-Service Performance."

[18] ICF, Inc., *Selected Use of Competition*, pp. III–16.

vider of medical services are the same firm, and there are no market transactions between the two. Any savings in utilization or cost accrues to this provider-insurer.

This identity between the insurer and provider is clear in the case of prepaid group practices. In the foundation model, the medical society or other organization that contracts to provide services is separate from the independent physicians who actually provide them. However, the physicians typically agree to subject themselves to strong financial penalties for unjustified rates of service provision (utilization) significantly above group norms. Such an arrangement is not a typical market purchase of services but a highly complex contract between a collective organization and its members. It is a third alternative for medical care transactions.

Returning to traditional insurance, market transactions between insurers and providers are made inefficient by moral hazard. Service benefit insurance, and indemnity benefits to a lesser extent, reduces the net price of medical services to the patient, making it in his interest to consume more and higher quality services than if he paid the full price. Acting as the patient's agent, the physician will direct the patient to utilize enough services so that an additional unit is barely worth as much as the net price.

Moral hazard entails a welfare loss to consumers as a group in terms of overuse of health care. The inefficiency shows up in higher medical care prices and utilization and therefore in higher insurance premiums. As first applied to health insurance by Pauly, "the incremental utilization of services from the lowering of net price is worth less to patients than the foregone resources (cost) used to produce the medical care."[19] In different language, patients are induced to utilize more medical care than is worthy of its cost.

The major virtue of combining the insurer and provider into one organization, or in developing a more complex contract between the two, is the reduction of the moral hazard that characterizes market transactions between insurers and consumers (or their agents, the physicians). When the provider is performing the insurance function, it is in his interest to ration patients' demand for services toward reduced utilization, as more of the fixed fee will be left as a residual for the provider. Indeed, it may be optimal to reduce utilization all the way back to the level that would occur with no insurance. Over time the fixed fee will decline to be consistent with this lower utilization level because of competition. At this level of utilization, the patient

---

[19] Mark V. Pauly, "The Economics of Moral Hazards: Comment," *American Economic Review*, vol. 68, no. 3 (June 1968), pp. 531–537.

receives an amount of service that maximizes consumer satisfaction. However, the risk-reduction benefits of health insurance are still present. To make the point in a different manner, utilization is discouraged by the provider so that the patient does not consume more health services as a result of insurance. Since the additional utilization is not worth the cost of the extra premium to the patient, he is pleased at the result of the provider's discouragement of utilization. Thus, the patient is likely to continue enrolling in the HMO.

In a sense, the HMO physician is performing a subtle shift in the agency relationship. Under traditional insurance arrangements, the physician-agent prescribes treatment on the basis of the price net of insurance that the patient must pay. In this case, the patient bears the cost of this moral hazard through higher premiums. However, when the provider is also the insurer, there is an incentive to use the agency relationship to prevent this from occurring. Here, the physician as the agent of the patient will not prescribe greater utilization simply because of insurance. Instead, a level of utilization that would be consistent with the patient's demands if the patient were to pay the full price is prescribed. Again, the result to the patient is the full risk-reduction benefits of insurance without the costs of excessive utilization.

The actual mechanics of physician-patient interaction in the HMO are not entirely clear. If the patient were entirely passive, one could envision the physician recommending the no-insurance level of utilization. Possibly, decisions on surgery are closest to this model since they are sufficiently technical that the patient is in the worst position to challenge them.

On the other hand, patients play a much more important role in the utilization of ambulatory care since they initiate most such visits. It is not clear how physicians discourage patients from overusing ambulatory care when the net price to the patient is either zero or nominal. Appointment queues and lengthier times between follow-up visits are some devices. But probably the more extensive patient role here means that a good part of ambulatory overutilization is not avoided. This may explain why studies comparing utilization in HMOs with populations with traditional health insurance benefits show substantially reduced hospital utilization but little if any reduction in ambulatory utilization.[20]

---

[20] If part of the reduction in hospital use represents substitution of ambulatory care, ambulatory use would increase unless it was discouraged. Also, deductibles for ambulatory care that are common in conventional insurance but absent in HMOs would lead to increased use. The fact that increased ambulatory use is either small or nonexistent implies substantial efforts to ration it in HMOs.

Thus, the ability of the physician to prevent the expansion of demand owing to the subsidy effect may depend on the relative roles of physicians and patients in decision making with regard to the utilization of various services.

Another issue that merits consideration is the nature of physician incentives to underdoctor. Most people would reason that physicians earn more money when they succeed at reducing utilization, and this is the driving incentive. However, incentives in many HMOs are not so simple. Typically, HMOs have large numbers of physicians, all of whom share the financial gains from the cost reduction efforts of a single physician.[21] This substantial dilution of the incentive is the "free-rider" problem, which characterizes many institutions in the economy. Both Pauly and the authors of this study have discussed it in the context of group medical practice.[22] Foundation-type HMOs have another problem with incentives besides the free-rider problem: there are private incentives to increase utilization.

Despite the difficulty of setting up strong financial incentives for individual physicians, group practice HMOs *can* reduce utilization of services in two ways. The physicians in the HMO can discuss and collectively determine criteria for medical care, especially for tonsillectomies, hysterectomies, and other surgical procedures. As a group, particularly if they are a partnership, they have the incentives to develop an efficient set of criteria. To the extent that such managerial criteria can apply to a large proportion of patients, the HMO can reduce utilization without strong incentives for the individual physician. Peer review can also perform this function. Compliance with agreed-on criteria can be monitored and pressure applied in situations where criteria are easy to establish beforehand. Another mechanism is the deliberate limitation of the number of hospital beds and/or physicians per patient. What some have argued was circumstance may be deliberate policy.[23]

The second manner in which group practice HMOs can reduce utilization is the simple absence of incentives that induce private fee-for-service practice to increase utilization. It is likely that in fee-for-service practice, physicians increase the demand for services beyond what would characterize the perfect agency relationship (see chapter

---

[21] According to a 1969 AMA survey, of those group practices where prepayment activity comprised more than 75 percent, 64 percent had twenty-six or more physicians. See C. Todd and M. E. McNamara, *Medical Groups in the United States, 1969* (Chicago: American Medical Association, 1971), p. 65.

[22] Mark V. Pauly, "Efficiency, Incentives and Reimbursement for Health Care," *Inquiry*, vol. 7, no. 2 (March 1970), pp. 114–131, and H. E. Frech III and Paul B. Ginsburg, "Optimal Scale in Medical Practice: A Survivor Analysis," *Journal of Business*, vol. 47, no. 1 (January 1974), pp. 23–36.

[23] Klarman, "Major Public Initiatives in Health."

3), for example, by suggesting extra visits or procedures that provide only a marginal benefit. This is another source of welfare losses in market transactions between providers and insurers that is eliminated by combining them into one organization.

To summarize, two types of moral hazard introduce inefficiency into transactions between providers and insurers. The provider may act as a perfect agent of the patient and order the extra medical care the patient desires as a result of the reduction of the net price to the patient. In addition, the provider may find that health insurance makes it easier to artificially increase demand for medical care. When the patient is not paying the bill, there will be less vigilance on his part as to how much medical care to purchase. In either case, resources are wasted because medical care is utilized up to a point where the value of additional care to the consumer is worth less than its cost.

The group practice HMO is an innovation that attempts to deal with this problem by internalizing insurer-provider transactions within a firm. Under this arrangement, incentives to shift demand toward greater utilization disappear, and incentives to reduce demand toward the uninsured level appear. The foundation-type HMO attempts to accomplish the same ends through a collective organization and administrative controls. Given the welfare loss resulting from the subsidy effect of health insurance, the HMO has the potential of substantially increasing economic efficiency and social welfare.

The choice between outside purchase of a service and internalizing the function within the firm is a familiar theme in the economics literature on firms and markets. In 1937 Coase pointed to transactions costs as the raison d'être of firms;[24] in simplest terms, certain transactions are performed more economically within a firm than between firms. Recently Williamson spelled out considerations dictating the extent to which transactions are made within the firm instead of across markets.[25] The problem here is an example of combining "opportunism," which he defines as a "lack of candor or honesty in transactions,"[26] with a small numbers exchange situation. In market transactions, opportunistic behavior is possible by physicians and patients mainly because of asymmetric information (they know more about the patient's health needs than the insurer does). By putting the physician in the same organization with the insurer, opportunistic behavior on his behalf is reduced, and a different type of opportunistic behavior is developed to counteract that of the patient.

---

[24] Ronald Coase, "The Nature of the Firm," *Economica*, vol. 4 (1937), pp. 386–405 (reprinted in many anthologies).

[25] Oliver E. Williamson, *Markets and Hierarchies* (New York: Free Press, 1975).

[26] Williamson, *Markets and Hierarchies*, p. 9.

With respect to service mix, one can argue that those services which are most sensitive to price will be those whose utilization is reduced the most in HMOs. But this would indicate that ambulatory care would be reduced more than hospital care, which is not the case. However, other factors are relevant here. The relative role of physician and patient decision making should make a difference. Utilization should be reduced most when physicians play a large role. Here, one expects hospitalization, and surgery in particular, to show the largest changes, and this is what has been occurring. Those services most subject to the establishment of uniform medical procedure would be most likely to be reduced. Finally, services most completely insured in the fee-for-service sector would have the greatest reductions.

Paying the HMO under Public Insurance

A question that has received little attention is how the public insurer should pay the HMO for services.[27] The answer depends upon the extent of public payment for HMO services and the proportion of an HMO's business that is subject to government payment.

Perhaps the simplest situation is one where the public insurer pays only for services for the poor and the elderly and will make payments only to HMOs in which the publicly supported patients are a minority of those enrolled. When government-supported patients are a small part of an HMO's business, the method of payment has little effect on resource allocation. Of course, if payments are less than costs public patients will not be served, but, if payments are equal to or greater than costs it is unlikely to matter much whether costs are reimbursed or flat capitation payments are made. The HMO is unlikely to be influenced by the incentives inherent in these reimbursement methods when a small proportion of its revenue is derived thus, and it might be unable, from legal restrictions or technical problems, to offer two grades of care.

If certain HMOs specialize in caring for those who are government-financed, the incentives of various payment methods must be taken into account. Under cost reimbursement arrangements, there is no incentive to control costs. Indeed, if profits are a percentage of costs or a generous return on assets, there will be incentives to inflate costs. Clearly, many of the advantages of HMOs would be lost under this type of financing.

An alternative method that is already in use is to pay a percentage of the costs of care in fee-for-service practice in the area, an arrange-

---

[27] An exception is Victor P. Goldberg, "Some Emerging Problems of Prepaid Health Plans in the Medical System," *Policy Analysis*, vol. 1, no. 1 (Winter 1975), pp. 55–68.

ment that maintains many HMO incentives since it is a capitation payment. The problem with it is that in view of HMO efficiency it may result in a much higher price than necessary. A high capitation payment would induce nonprice competition, leading to "goldplated" HMO service. Since each publicly supported patient would be highly profitable, HMOs would work to attract them. With price competition ruled out, the only options available would be increasing amenities and marketing efforts. Initial windfall profits would be transformed into amenities and selling costs.

The most feasible method of paying HMOs where public patients comprise a substantial part of the membership would be to base capitation payments on the cost experience of a group of HMOs. This would retain the HMO incentives without generating a windfall that could lead to resource waste in the long run. Such a proposal is similar to current reform proposals for nursing home reimbursement, where public patients are in a majority in most institutions.[28]

The problems multiply when all people have NHI benefits and are served by HMOs. In the abstract, such an arrangement makes little sense. Since the crucial aspect of the HMO is its acting as an insurer as well as a provider, the role of the public insurer is necessarily quite limited. The government can buy HMO membership for the poor and deal with adverse selection problems, but it accomplishes little and may do great harm to incentives in buying HMO membership for those who are willing and able to buy it for themselves.[29]

Nevertheless, such a situation could occur as a result of the long transition from fee-for-service to HMOs. Only about 5 million people in the United States are served by HMOs at present, and even if this type of organization became instantly popular with physicians and patients, a long period of time would have to elapse before it became dominant. Since a separate health insurance policy (whether private or public) is needed to reduce financial risks under fee-for-service medicine, it is likely that under the comprehensive NHI proposals, a public insurance system will already be in place by the time HMOs predominate. For this reason, the government would end up paying a large proportion of HMO premiums.

With government as the major financer of HMO service, the problem of level of care must be faced. As before, it makes little sense to

[28] See Paul B. Ginsburg, "Cost Containment through Reform of Nursing Home Reimbursement," in Selma Mushkin, ed., *Academia and State Health Policy Issues* (Washington, D.C.: Public Services Laboratory, Georgetown University, 1976), pp. 25–46, for a review of the issues and complexities of these proposals.

[29] Some NHI proposals covering all citizens simply require employer purchases of insurance. Since a large part of the population might already have such insurance, NHI would not affect them unless changes in benefits were required.

reimburse HMOs on the basis of incurred costs. This eliminates desirable HMO incentives and at a stroke turns these organizations into quasi-fee-for-service providers. Clearly, a set annual premium must be paid. But at what level? It could be the mean of HMO costs across an area. However, unless extra charges are allowed, this policy precludes individuals from exercising any choice as to the expensiveness of care they will obtain. A more serious problem is that the dynamic implications for the level of care are not clear. If competition induces those below the mean to increase amenities and other aspects of care while those above the mean do the opposite, there might be no movement in the level of care over time. Thus, a major policy decision would be made by default. The level of care would be the mean at a point in time and the payment system would maintain it.

An alternative is payment by the government of a fee to cover the costs of basic care, with HMOs able to charge an extra fee for "luxury" care. This would get around the problem of uniform levels of care. The public insurer could subtract supplementary payments from HMO costs to obtain the mean costs of basic care. Again, government might want to exercise more discretion in setting reimbursement for basic care, since judgments as to the best level may change over time. It is important that the basic level of care be set below that chosen by most consumers. In that way wasteful government purchase of better care than consumers prefer is avoided.[30]

HMOs and Competition

HMOs are likely to change the nature of the market for medical care toward greater competition. Considering the large number of independent physicians practicing in any given urban area, one might expect the market for physician services to approximate pure competition.[31] However, as we have argued, this is not the case. Because information about quality, amenity level, and price are difficult to obtain, each physician has monopoly power.

The presence of HMOs in the market for medical services can either

---

[30] See Paul B. Ginsburg, "Regulating the Price of Hospital Care," in Thomas G. Moore, ed., *Regulatory Reform* (Washington, D.C.: American Enterprise Institute, forthcoming), for a discussion of determining the quality of care by setting the regulated rate and the difficulties of making such a decision in hospitals.

[31] One departure from competition is that entry into the profession is restricted by licensure. One must graduate from an accredited medical school to be licensed, and the number of accredited schools (and the number of openings in them) is tightly controlled by the AMA. See H. E. Frech III, "Occupational Licensure and Health Care Productivity," in John A. Rafferty, ed., *Health Manpower and Productivity* (Lexington, Mass.: Heath, 1975), pp. 112–132.

monopolize it further, by reducing the number of competitors, or increase competition by providing information. Since HMOs tend to be large, a large number of people become aware of their amenity levels, prices, and quality of care. This results in an increased likelihood of choices of provider being made on the basis of price and quality comparisons. We suspect that the additional information is substantially more important than the decline in the number of competitors, at least in urban areas. When this is the case, the net result is a more competitive market.

6

Policy Implications

The analysis reported here has some significant implications for the design of national health insurance in the United States. These implications are spelled out below, but it must be recognized that no complete policy analysis of NHI is intended. Instead, we point out where the analysis of the relationship between public insurance and privately provided medical services is relevant to an issue and might influence its resolution in one direction or another. Other considerations not brought out here could lead one to decide an issue in the opposite direction.

Extent of Population Coverage

While the most frequently stated rationale for NHI is to increase access to medical services by the poor, many of the proposals introduced into Congress call for coverage for the entire population. There are a number of advantages to such a plan. First, it is likely to be easier to administer, since judgments on eligibility will not have to be made. Indeed, the complexity of the definition of eligibility for Medicaid is often cited as a major administrative weakness. Second, universal coverage eliminates problems with the cutoff point. If the income cutoff is not carefully designed to gradually reduce the subsidy received, severe work disincentives are created. This is a major problem with current welfare programs, including Medicaid. A third advantage is that as a vehicle to increase planning and regulation of the medical care system, NHI is more influential the greater the proportion of the population covered (see above, chapter 2).

A fourth reason for covering the entire population involves, ironically, access by the poor. When only the poor are covered, it is tempting in light of budgetary problems to reduce rates of reimbursement for medical care, as a number of states did during the recent recession. As a result, those insured by the government program would have difficulty obtaining care. Payments so low as to seriously reduce access are less likely under universal coverage because political pressure is likely to keep payment levels up and because providers have no better-paying patients to turn to.

There are some serious disadvantages to covering the entire population, however, especially if the plan calls for little cost sharing by the patient. One of these occurs if taxes are used to finance the system and thus must be increased. Since taxes involve loss of consumer welfare through distortion of incentives to work and invest, the tax system is a very costly source of financing of medical care for the bulk of the population. Voluntary payment of health insurance premiums causes no such distortion. Two additional disadvantages of complete coverage flow directly from the analysis in this monograph. First, health insurance of any kind has important side effects, leading to overconsumption of medical care in terms of quantity, quality, and amenities. A major rationale for NHI is to enable the poor to purchase more medical services than they would otherwise, but there is no basis for extending this logic to the entire population.

Numerous writers have pointed to the fact that the marginal health benefits of increased medical care are very small (see also Appendix A). Indeed, one recent writer claims that they are negative.[1] It would be folly to finance a substantial increase in the utilization of health services by the bulk of the population, because the resources that it would take are valued more highly elsewhere. Because of the present tax subsidy to the purchase of excessive health insurance, many have argued that the nonpoor population in the United States is already devoting more of its resources to medical care than it really wants to. Less complete insurance and less medical care would benefit the nonpoor because resources would be freed up for other goods and services. Coverage of the entire population under NHI could aggravate the problem of excessive resource diversion to health care while doing little for the poor, since many are now covered by Medicaid and Medicare. Coverage of the entire population by health maintenance organizations or other private third-party payers with cost control incentives would mitigate some of these problems. However, such a far-reaching institutional change seems unlikely.

In addition to the negative implications of complete coverage in

---

[1] Ivan Illych, *Medical Nemesis: The Expropriation of Health* (New York: Pantheon, 1976).

inducing overutilization of medical care at quality and amenity levels that are too high, the additional insurance would also drive up prices. Further, the presence of at least some forms of public insurance would reduce consumer incentives to search for the best price/quality combination, leading to additional insulation of individual providers from market forces and thus to further inefficiency and higher prices. The larger the population covered by relatively complete insurance, the more aggravated these problems of waste of resources and monopoly gains to providers will be. In fact, if the entire population is covered with complete insurance, the market for medical care would be completely eliminated as an allocative and price-setting mechanism. Detailed planning and regulation would have to take its place.

A second unfavorable effect of complete coverage raised by this analysis is an increase in the difficulty of regulation. We noted above that with full coverage insurance, regulation of reimbursements would be necessary for private provision of services. Even with indemnity insurance, the public insurer must set the level of the indemnity payments—a type of regulatory function. If only a small part of the population is covered by public insurance, there are ample guides in market data to set these prices. But when the proportion of medical care paid for by NHI becomes large, the prices obtained by providers in the market are no longer a worthwhile guide because they are influenced by the presence of public insurance. Indeed, if the market sector were very small it is conceivable and even likely that automatic adjustment of regulated prices on the basis of market data would lead to inflation.

If market prices cannot be used, it is not clear what can take their place. In the short run, prices can be increased from pre-NHI levels according to general inflation in the economy. However, this is only appropriate for the short run, as it does not allow relative prices to change. There is a potential trial and error mechanism, but it is highly cumbersome. After setting prices, one could look for evidence of excess supply or excess demand and revise the price accordingly. However, this is difficult and costly to measure.[2] When such a process of responding to shortages and surpluses is not formalized, one might call it "muddling through." Thus, coverage of the entire population makes the combination of public financing and private provision less tenable.

---

[2] Note the discussion in Appendix A of Held and Reinhardt's finding that "shortage" areas designated by the Department of Health, Education, and Welfare have easier physician access than other nonmetropolitan counties. See also Phillip J. Held and Uwe Reinhardt, "Health Manpower Policy in a Market Context," paper presented at the annual meeting of the American Economic Association, Dallas, Texas, December 27–30, 1975.

Indemnity versus Service Benefit Insurance

Both service and indemnity benefits are currently used by private insurers in the United States today. The analysis here has shown some clear advantages for indemnity insurance[3] but only one major advantage of service benefits. The latter are easier to administer. Simply defining a coinsurance percentage and the types of services to which it applies suffices to set up a service benefit scheme. For indemnity insurance, a dollar reimbursement level per covered service must be set. This is clearly more difficult, particularly in an inflationary economy when the reimbursement rate must be revised periodically. A minor advantage of service benefit insurance is that more risk is eliminated for the consumer. Under indemnity benefits, the consumer undertakes the risk that the price of care he receives might sometimes be higher than the indemnity benefit by an amount greater than the coinsurance payment he would make under service benefits. If so, the difference must be paid out of pocket. Under service benefits, where the consumer pays a fixed percentage of the bill whatever it is, there is less risk of absorbing a large expense for services from a high-priced provider. There are ways in which these risks can be reduced, as discussed above in chapter 3, but the disadvantage remains.

The advantages of indemnity benefits, however, seem more important. Essentially, indemnity benefits enable the purposes of NHI to be accomplished at lower costs and with less waste than do service benefits. As we showed in chapter 3, for a given quantity of medical care, the market price would be lower under indemnity benefits than under service benefits. This is the result of a reduction in monopoly gains that providers are able to obtain. In addition to restricting the extent of the transfer from taxpayers to providers, indemnity benefits eliminate some of the incentives inherent in service benefits to purchase too much in the way of quality and amenities. Under service benefits, if the consumer desires to pay more for a more desirable provider, insurance will pay most of the difference. Under indemnity insurance, the consumer pays the full price of upgrading and thus will weigh the full cost against the added benefit. This reduces overuse of resources in health care. Finally, since indemnity benefits do not eliminate incentives to search, consumers will be better informed and more responsive to price differences, making medical care markets more competitive.

---

[3] Frech and Ginsburg have argued that extensive use of service benefits by Blue Cross and Blue Shield plans may be a deliberate attempt to increase the incomes of providers who control these plans. See H. E. Frech III, "The Regulation of Health Insurance," (Ph.D. diss., University of California, Los Angeles, 1974), pp. 46–67, and Frech and Ginsburg, "Competition among Health Insurers," pp. 4–5.

Extra Charges above Regulated Fees

The answer to the issue of extra charges over a regulated price is not clear-cut: it depends on the extensiveness of NHI coverage. The argument for prohibiting extra charges goes like this: if providers have monopoly power, regulating prices can be effective and nonprice rationing will not be necessary. The effect will be a transfer of some monopoly gains from providers to taxpayers. However, this equity argument for prohibiting extra charges looks less promising as other aspects are considered. For one thing, if only the poor are covered by NHI, problems of access may develop as providers choose to spend their time on patients who will pay their full fees.[4] In addition providers may respond to the limitation on fees by reducing the quality of their care and the level of amenities. Thus, the complex regulation may be unsuccessful at capturing much of the monopoly gains for consumers and may in fact wind up driving quality to a low level.

Third, the level of the regulated fee would probably be set so low that less of the service would be supplied than demanded. If the market is not permitted to clear, various nonprice rationing devices will crop up to reduce the amount demanded to the quantity supplied. Many of these techniques are costly, such as waiting in line. Another reaction to excess demand is that some providers may decide to give services to attractive people who live in pleasant locations. As we have argued above, nonprice rationing allows suppliers to alter many features of medical care without concern for the effect on consumer satisfaction, and the poor would suffer most under such a rationing scheme. Additionally, the provider might decide to limit those services to illnesses that are regarded as either important or interesting. To the extent the provider is altruistic, the rationing process will not have such unfortunate effects. But even then, providers are not aware of what *consumers* consider important, particularly when a large proportion of medical services amount to subjective caring rather than objective curing.

If providers are allowed to make extra charges, the market for medical services will clear and access will not be denied to beneficiaries of public programs. Also, quality will not decline to a low level. Under

---

[4] This has been the unfortunate experience of Medicaid in providing access to physician services. A recent study of Medicaid's Early Periodic Screening, Diagnosis, and Treatment Program documents the absence of treatment of those conditions detected by screening because of refusal by local physicians to treat Medicaid patients. See *Medicaid for the Young* (Atlanta: Southern Regional Council, 1976). Representative John E. Moss (D–Calif.) stated that "mismanagement . . . of this program has caused unnecessary crippling, retardation, or even death of thousands of children" (*New York Times*, December 9, 1976).

these rules, the system would become, in effect, one of indemnity insurance, enjoying the advantages of this form of insurance reviewed above.

However, there is one serious problem with allowing extra charges that we have yet to take up. It is the poor who would have most difficulty paying the extra charges and thus be more frequently rationed out of the market by price than would the rest of the population.[5] Thus, a major purpose of NHI might not be realized.

There are a number of possible solutions to this problem. First, only the poor could be covered under NHI, concentrating all the subsidy or increase in purchasing power in the poorer segment of society. This arrangement would also permit higher indemnity payments or lower cost sharing in service benefits, as there would not be such a concern with high tax burdens and allocating too many resources to health. Thus, there are important connections between the coverage decision and methods of reimbursement.

A second option is to vary cost sharing with income. It would accomplish part of what covering only the poor would accomplish. Income-related cost sharing might be more politically acceptable, would eliminate the abrupt termination of benefits with a rise in income, and could be easily integrated with a catastrophic protection program. However, the size of the administrative problems with such a scheme are not clear. A final option is to set very high levels of reimbursement. However, this is very wasteful as it encourages maximum overutilization and the maximum increase of monopoly gains to providers. To conclude, concentrating the program on the poor holds the best prospects of avoiding the many allocative problems with disallowing extra payments above the regulated level while ensuring that the program aims of providing access to medical care by the poor are achieved.

The Role of HMOs

Health maintenance organizations have the potential of improving the efficiency of the medical care market by integrating insurers and providers and thereby creating incentives for the providers to control costs. A particular advantage is that virtually complete insurance is possible without destroying the ability of the market to allocate resources. This gives HMOs a particularly useful role to play if coverage is universal. Of course, if HMOs become more widespread, providing the middle class with extensive insurance coverage without the usual concomitant costs

---

[5] It is possible that the poor would receive care from low-quality providers rather than not at all. This might be acceptable if one interprets the public mandate as a minimum level of care to all rather than equality of care. However, the range of prices in which this solution occurs might be extremely narrow.

of overutilization, the clamor for NHI could be reduced to one of buying the poor into HMOs. With mixed (poor and nonpoor) membership, some of the problems in using the HMO as a vehicle for health care for the poor might be alleviated.[6]

The immediate problem with regard to HMOs is to reverse current policies that discourage them. There is a long history of state laws hostile to the development of HMOs,[7] and while federal policy became officially favorable with the passage in 1973 of the Health Maintenance Organization Act, one may suspect that the law was written by interests hostile to HMOs. Little help has actually been rendered and some provisions of that law are, indeed, harmful to the continued existence of HMOs.[8]

Considering more positive policies, start-up assistance to HMOs is justified by the weak state of capital markets for nonprofit organizations. Medicare regulations could be changed to increase incentives for HMOs to enroll the elderly. One of the authors was told by an HMO consultant that under present regulations HMOs were better off billing Medicare on a fee-for-service basis than contracting for prepaid services. At the very least, the regulatory and reimbursement system should be neutral to HMOs.

The Role of Deductibles

An approach to NHI that differs from most of the bills introduced into Congress has been developed independently by Martin Feldstein and Mark Pauly.[9] Under these proposals, the federal government provides insurance with an income-related deductible. The deductible becomes large for the nonpoor, so that for most of the population, the proposal can be considered one that covers catastrophic expenses only. The plan meets the goals of subsidizing the poor and alleviating the apparent market failure with regard to catastrophic insurance, but does not

---

[6] Victor P. Goldberg, "Some Emerging Problems of Prepaid Health Plans in the Medical System," *Policy Analysis*, vol. 1, no. 1 (Winter 1975).

[7] H. E. Frech III, "The Case of the Medical Care Industry," in Thomas G. Moore, ed., *Regulatory Reform* (Washington, D.C.: American Enterprise Institute, forthcoming).

[8] The major problem has been high minimum standards for comprehensiveness of insured services, standards above the norms for the private health insurance policies that HMOs must compete with. Paul Starr, "The Undelivered Health System," *The Public Interest*, vol. 42, no. 1 (Winter 1976), pp. 66–85.

[9] See Martin Feldstein, "A New Approach to National Health Insurance," *Public Interest*, no. 23 (Spring 1971), pp. 99–105, and Mark V. Pauly, *National Health Insurance: An Analysis* (Washington, D.C.: American Enterprise Institute, 1971), pp. 33–41, for discussions of major risk insurance and variable subsidy insurance, and for their respective proposals.

add insurance coverage for the nonpoor. In fact, less insurance for small losses of the nonpoor is envisioned. Of all the proposals for NHI, this one does most to strengthen the market in allocating resources.

However, the problem with these proposals is that they leave untouched the substantial tax subsidies to the purchase of private health insurance. Health insurance purchase has been found to be highly sensitive to price,[10] and because of the tax deductibility of this insurance (to employees receiving it as a fringe benefit and to people purchasing their own insurance), there is a strong incentive to purchase it extensively. With general inflation pushing people into higher tax brackets, the subsidy is becoming larger over time. Feldstein's and Pauly's visions of people dropping private insurance in favor of catastrophic insurance will not be borne out unless such subsidies are removed. Given the tax distortions, the rational individual might indeed buy a private policy that covers the deductible and coinsurance of a government program and have effective full coverage. This purchase perpetuates the moral hazard that the public program is designed to curtail. Tax deductibility for health insurance should be eliminated. If supplementary insurance continued to be a problem, it could easily be taxed.

Elimination of the ever-growing tax subsidy to the purchase of insurance is essential to a rational system for financing medical care. Unfortunately, there are important vested interests in its maintenance—insurance companies, hospitals, physicians, and individuals benefiting from the tax subsidies. Individuals can be bought off by allowing them a tax deduction (or tax credit) comparable in size to current health insurance deductions but not linked to the purchase of health insurance. Possibly one could call it an employment tax incentive.

Indeed, with the elimination of subsidies to the purchase of private health insurance, the structure of private insurance would resemble that provided by the government under the Feldstein and Pauly proposals. The government would still have to subsidize the poor, but

---

[10] See Bridger Mitchell and Ronald Vogel, "Health and Taxes: An Assessment of the Medical Deduction," *Southern Economic Journal*, vol. 41 (April 1975), and Martin S. Feldstein and Elizabeth Allison, "Tax Subsidies of Private Health Insurance: Distribution, Revenue Loss and Effects," in *The Economics of Federal Subsidy Programs* (Washington, D.C.: U.S. Congress, Joint Economic Committee, 1974), for discussion of the substantial size of the tax subsidy resulting from the tax exemption of employer health insurance premiums. See Charles E. Phelps, *Demand for Health Insurance: A Theoretical and Empirical Investigation* (Santa Monica: Rand, 1973), for estimates of the price elasticity of the demand for health insurance. The elasticity of the proportion of bills paid by the insurer with respect to the price of insurance (premiums divided by expected benefits) was found to be approximately −1.55.

with growing purchase of private insurance with catastrophic maximums taking place already, middle- and upper-income people would buy insurance with large deductibles, coinsurance, and indemnity features and therefore pay more out of pocket for routine medical care. Given the potential cost control capabilities of private health insurers, along with the greater range of consumer choice, this would probably be a very desirable outcome.

APPENDIX A

The Approach: Economic Analysis of Health Care

Economic analysis can contribute to the understanding of health policy issues. By this we do not mean that health care should be analyzed as if it were wheat, hats, or electricity. Health care has characteristics that differentiate it from many other goods—technical ignorance by consumers, existence of nonprofit providers, and extensive government intervention, to name a few. Indeed the characteristics differentiating health care get top attention in economic analyses of health care.

We regard health services as an appropriate topic for economic analysis, first, because prices (costs) play a role in decisions made with regard to producing and consuming them, and second, because these prices (costs) have policy relevance. The remainder of this appendix elaborates on these two points.

Consumer Needs and Demand. The most significant debate with respect to the role of prices has focused on the demand side. It is sometimes argued that health care decisions are commonly made under stress and in life-threatening situations. The patient is hopelessly ignorant of the technology of medical care and thus surrenders discretion to the physician. The physician in turn decides on a treatment solely on the basis of professional assessment of need. Under this scenario, price and cost are irrelevant to utilization decisions. In economists' parlance, the demand function is price inelastic.

While this scenario has surface plausibility, it breaks down under closer scrutiny. Most medical decisions do not deal with life-threatening situations. Econometric studies of the relationship between increments of medical care and population mortality show that the contribution of increases in medical care to health status is quite small.[1] Studies

---

[1] The focus of these studies is not on what the health status of the population would be if no medical care were delivered, but rather the effect that increases or decreases from the present level have on health status. Examples of such studies

by epidemiologists show that many medical procedures have little effect on life expectancy.[2] As Victor Fuchs summarizes the evidence:

> Medical intervention has a significant effect on outcome in only a small fraction of cases seen by the average physician. Most illnesses are self-limiting: they will run their course and disappear. . . . Many others are chronic: given the present limits of medical knowledge, they are incurable.[3]

We interpret these findings to imply that many of the benefits of medical care are subjective. They include alleviation of symptoms, reduction of anxiety, and greater comfort. Fuchs distinguishes between "caring" and "curing" and speaks of the demand for caring.[4]

While the reduction in anxiety and symptomatic relief are valuable benefits of medical care, these should be treated differently from life-saving benefits. Specifically, the caring function of medicine makes understandable the fact that price influences demand. People are willing to make trade-offs between the subjective benefits of medicine and the benefits that they derive from other goods and services. If a large portion of medical care improves the quality of life but not objectively measurable health status or life expectancy, the usefulness of the concept of "need" is called into question. An example from dentistry shows this point.

Some adults are faced with the choice of expensive root canal work or the possible loss of teeth. Replacement of teeth with dentures is a less costly but less comfortable alternative. While dentists might maintain that root canal work is "needed" for these patients, one can certainly imagine people opting for better housing, more leisure, or a child's college education over costly dental work. In such an instance, the price of dental care is likely to affect utilization. A medical example would be coronary bypass surgery. While a reduction in angina pain is an accepted result, there has been no hard evidence that the proce-

---

include Richard Auster, Irving Leveson, and Deborah Sarachek, "The Production of Health: An Exploratory Study," *Journal of Human Resources*, vol. 5, no. 3 (Fall 1969), pp. 411–436; Charles Stewart, "Allocation of Resources to Health," *Journal of Human Resources*, vol. 6, no. 1 (Winter 1971), pp. 103–122; and Lee Benham and Alexandra Benham, "The Impact of Incremental Medical Services on Health Status, 1964–1970," in Ronald Andersen, Joanna Kravits, and Odin Anderson, eds., *Equity in Health Services: Empirical Analysis in Social Policy* (Cambridge, Mass.: Ballinger, 1975).

[2] Many of these studies are reviewed in Archibald Cochrane, *Effectiveness and Efficiency* (London: Nuffield Provincial Hospital's Trust, 1971).

[3] Victor R. Fuchs, *Who Shall Live? Health, Economics, and Social Choice* (New York: Basic Books, 1974), p. 64.

[4] Ibid., p. 65.

dure prolongs life, except in the 2 or 3 percent of bypasses done where all arteries leading to the heart are damaged.

Few would deny that medical care is technologically complex and that the patient's information tends to be limited. However, this does not eliminate opportunities for discretion by the patient. Feldstein's view of the physician as the patient's agent is useful here.[5] The physician provides information as to diagnostic procedures and treatment and referral to appropriate medical services, including his own. If this agency relationship is perfect, the physician will act as if he were "in the patient's shoes," combining technical knowledge with the patient's attitudes toward health, pain, disability, and financial costs. If the agency relationship were exact, the role of the physician could be ignored in studying the demand for medical care, since the behavior would correspond to the case where the patient chooses using perfect technical information.

But of course, the agency relationship is imperfect. Consumers are unlikely to recognize all decisions made that are not in their interest. Physicians probably have a bias toward decisions that emphasize more extensive use of professional services, either from pecuniary motives or simply from the shortcomings of medical training which tend to emphasize doing all that is possible for the patient regardless of cost. The literature is replete with assertions that by giving misleading advice, physicians may shift the demand for their services.[6] However, as long as consumers have limited private wealth and insurance is not complete, utilization of medical services will be responsive to the extent of insurance coverage (the major influence on prices to the patient) and the patient's income.[7] There may be a bias toward overdoctoring at all levels of insurance coverage, but fee-for-service utilization will still be responsive to the consumer out-of-pocket price.

Empirical research based on two different approaches has confirmed this view. One approach has been to measure utilization changes over time in groups whose insurance coverage has changed. While it is best to have a control group whose insurance coverage has not changed, "natural" experiments of this type are rare. The best-known

---

[5] See Martin Feldstein, "Econometric Studies of Health Economics," in Michael Intrilligator and David Kendrick, eds., *Frontiers of Quantitative Economics*, vol. 2 (Amsterdam: North-Holland, 1974), pp. 377–447.

[6] Robert G. Evans, "Supplier-Induced Demand: Some Empirical Evidence and Implications," in Mark Perlman, ed., *The Economics of Health and Medical Care*, pp. 162–173; Mark V. Pauly, "The Role of Demand Creation in the Provision of Health Services," paper presented to the annual meeting of the American Economic Association, Dallas, Texas, December 30, 1975; and Feldstein, "Econometric Studies."

[7] This enters the utility function in Pauly's model. See Pauly, "The Role of Demand Creation."

recent study of this type is that of Scitovsky and Snyder, who found that the change from full coverage for physician services to 25 percent coinsurance in a Stanford University employee plan reduced physician visits by 25 percent.[8]

The other approach has been statistical analysis of cross-sectional data, including state aggregates as well as survey data on families. While estimates have ranged widely, all studies find a negative effect of price on use.[9] Since health insurance coverage is the major source of variation in prices (to the patient) of medical services, one can predict that the extent of coverage would affect the demand for, and thus the utilization of, health services.

While the studies of health insurance and the demand for medical care have been useful in establishing and measuring sensitivity of medical care utilization to price, they have for the most part restricted themselves to quantities of services, such as hospital days or physician visits, but have ignored the quality dimension. Quality means different things to different people. To most, it encompasses the absence of errors in medical diagnosis and treatment. To some, it also includes the intensity or sophistication of treatment. Those who have studied rising hospital costs note that a major reason for this phenomenon is the changing nature of a day of care.[10] Each year, the typical hospital day involves

[8] Anne Scitovsky and Nelda Snyder, "Effects of Coinsurance on Physician Services," *Social Security Bulletin*, vol. 35, no. 6 (June 1972), pp. 3–19. Older studies of this type are critically reviewed in Paul B. Ginsburg and Lawrence M. Manheim, "Insurance Copayment and Health Services Utilization," *Journal of Economics and Business*, vol. 25 (Spring-Summer 1973).

[9] The more important of these studies include Martin S. Feldstein, "Hospital Cost Inflation: A Study of Nonprofit Price Dynamics," *American Economic Review*, vol. 61 (December 1971); Rosett and Huang, "Effect of Health Insurance"; Victor R. Fuchs and Marcia J. Kramer, *Determinants of Expenditures for Physicians' Services in the United States, 1948–1968* (New York: National Bureau of Economic Research, 1973); and Joseph P. Newhouse and Charles E. Phelps, "New Estimates of Price and Income Elasticities of Medical Care Services," in Richard N. Rosett, ed., *The Role of Health Insurance in the Health Services Sector* (New York: National Bureau of Economic Research, 1976), pp. 261–312. Newhouse and Phelps, "New Estimates of Elasticities," p. 312, obtained lower estimates of elasticities than the other studies (−.33 for hospital care and −.22 for physician services at the mean coinsurance rate for each). They criticized the other studies on econometric grounds in *On Having Your Cake and Eating It Too*, arguing that the earlier estimates are too high because of biases in estimation.

[10] For example, Martin S. Feldstein, *The Rising Cost of Hospital Care* (Washington, D.C.: Information Resources Press, 1971); Michael Redisch "Hospital Inflationary Mechanisms," paper presented at Western Economic Association meeting, Las Vegas, Nevada, June 10–12, 1974; David P. Baron, "A Study of Hospital Cost Inflation," *Journal of Human Resources*, vol. 9, no. 1 (Winter 1974), pp. 33–49; and Karen Davis, "The Role of Technology, Demand, and Labor Markets in the Determination of Hospital Costs," in Perlman, ed., *Economics of Health and Medical Care*, pp. 283–301.

more ancillary services such as laboratory tests and radiology procedures. The study of this aspect of the quality dimension is clearly important to cost containment policies. A final dimension of quality is the amenities connected with the service—waiting time, pleasant surroundings, good food, congenial, supportive personnel, and so on.

None of the studies of medical care utilization discussed above has examined the demand for quality.[11] However, note that an insurance plan that covers all or part of the *extra* cost of higher quality (service benefit insurance) would induce people to seek out those providers offering the high quality services. Alternatively, as Feldstein has suggested, providers might seize upon the opportunity presented by increased health insurance to raise quality (and prices) without suffering a reduced demand for output.[12] Evidence for the importance of the phenomenon of insuring increasing quality comes from studies of hospital cost inflation. Davis and Baron have shown in analyses of micro data on samples of hospitals over a period of years that demand factors, especially expanding insurance, are responsible for an important part of increases in hospital costs.[13] Feldstein found a similar result with state aggregate data.[14] It is likely that the impact of insurance on the "quality" of care is a more important determinant of increases in medical expenditures than its effect on quantity.

Provider Behavior. Health care is provided by a wide variety of sources, including hospitals and nursing homes (both proprietary and nonprofit), independent physicians, groups of physicians, and home health workers. We focus on independent physicians and argue that the analysis applies in an approximate sense to all other providers of health services. Physician influence extends far beyond their offices. As the patient's agent, they determine the nature of the services demanded from other medical providers as well as from themselves. Indeed some analysts go so far as to claim that physicians collectively have effective control over the hospitals in which they practice.[15] Thus, a model of physician behavior can be seen as a simplified model of the entire medical care system.

---

[11] An exception is Martin S. Feldstein, "Quality Change and the Demand for Hospital Care," *Econometrica*, forthcoming. In an extension of his earlier study, "Hospital Cost Inflation," Feldstein uses hospital inputs per unit of care as a quality measure. He finds that higher "quality" increases the demand for admissions.

[12] Feldstein, "Hospital Cost Inflation," p. 855.

[13] Davis, "Role of Technology, Demand, and Labor Markets in the Determination of Hospital Costs," and Baron, "Study of Hospital Cost Inflation."

[14] Feldstein, "Hospital Cost Inflation," p. 870.

[15] Mark Pauly and Michael Redisch, "The Not-for-Profit Hospital as a Physicians' Cooperative," *American Economic Review*, vol. 63, no. 1 (March 1973), pp. 87–99.

Furthermore, NHI will affect the market for physician services more than the market for hospital services. This is due to the already existing extensive coverage of hospital services by private insurance and the Medicare and Medicaid programs. In fiscal year 1972, 90 percent of inpatient hospital expenses were covered by third parties, while only 60 percent of expenses for outpatient physicians' services were so covered.[16] For hospital care, most proposals for NHI essentially replace private with public insurance of similar benefit structure, or require private insurance policies similar to those in use today. On the other hand, a substantial increase in coverage for outpatient physicians' services is contemplated in many NHI proposals.

A final reason for focusing on one type of provider, in this case physicians, is that results obtained for one category are often relevant to the others. For example, if one is investigating the effect of an increase in the demand for hospital services, the hypothesis that output will increase is corroborated under profit maximization and under a host of nonprofit behavioral assumptions. While hospitals of different types will differ at a point in time, their qualitative reaction to changes in their economic and regulatory environment is often the same.[17] Thus, the argument we make about physicians will apply to other providers also.

In modeling the behavior of physicians, it is important to consider the objectives that physicians pursue in making decisions about pricing, output, amenities, and other variables. A variety of models have been used by economists to study physician behavior. The simplest is profit maximization. This model initially assumes that physicians behave like other enterprises. However, when ethical and regulatory constraints are introduced, the model becomes more specific to medical care. Evidence of short-run behavior of physicians does not at first glance appear to be consistent with the profit maximization model: prices are infrequently changed and it is claimed that queues are often allowed to develop. Such behavior can be explained by the costliness of frequent price changes and regulatory restrictions imposed by insurers and government payers. One would not expect these considerations to be relevant over longer periods of time.

---

[16] Joseph Newhouse, Charles Phelps, and William Schwartz, "Policy Options and the Impact of National Health Insurance," *New England Journal of Medicine*, vol. 290, no. 24 (June 13, 1974), pp. 1345–1359.

[17] For more on this point, see Mark V. Pauly, "The Behavior of Nonprofit Hospital Monopolies: Alternative Models of the Hospital," in Clark C. Havighurst, ed., *Regulating Health Facilities Construction* (Washington, D.C.: American Enterprise Institute, 1974), pp. 143–162.

There is evidence, however, that nonprice rationing by physicians in the form of long waits for appointments and refusal to accept new patients is actually quite rare, in spite of common beliefs on the subject. A recently reported telephone survey of physicians reported waits to appointment of established patients of 3.20 days in large metropolitan areas, 5.97 days in small metropolitan areas, and 4.89 days in nonmetropolitan areas. The percentage of physicians not accepting new patients was 7.00 percent, 6.58 percent and 3.21 percent respectively. Particularly interesting was that access was *better* in rural counties considered to have a shortage of medical resources by the U.S. Department of Health, Education, and Welfare than in nonmetropolitan counties in general.[18]

There are many variations of the profit-maximizing model, some of which are important. One takes leisure into account explicitly. Physicians maximize satisfaction from income and leisure. As medical hourly earnings increase, hours worked could decline. This model may have empirical relevance, as Sloan found that physician hours decline as their hourly earnings increase.[19] However, a decline in hours worked by physicians need not imply a decline in output. Physicians can substitute lesser skilled personnel such as nurses, physician assistants, and technicians as their own time becomes relatively more valuable. Thus, the output increase from an increase in demand predicted by the profit-maximizing model is likely also to occur under the income-leisure model—at least in the long run.[20]

Other variations of these models exist. Feldstein alleges that physicians value interesting patients and income—thus causing a shortage of care for uninteresting cases.[21] In the hospital sector, it is likely that prices have adjusted for this, as hospitals tend to lose money on the more interesting cases and generate surpluses on routine care, leading one to believe that there are no shortages after all. Feldstein's argu-

---

[18] Phillip J. Held and Uwe Reinhardt, "Health Manpower Policy in a Market Context," paper presented at the annual meeting of the American Economic Association, Dallas, Texas, December 27–30, 1975.

[19] Frank A. Sloan, "A Microanalysis of Physicians' Hours of Work." Sloan obtained this result using data on individual physicians and state aggregates. However, he is unsure of the reliability of his results as he was unable to find a significant income effect from nonwage income.

[20] Uwe Reinhardt, "A Production Function for Physician Services," *Review of Economics and Statistics*, vol. 54, no. 1 (February 1972), pp. 55–66. Reinhardt found unexploited opportunities for the substitution of nonphysician personnel for physicians in office practice.

[21] Martin S. Feldstein, "The Rising Price of Physician Services," *Review of Economics and Statistics*, vol. 52, no. 2 (May 1970).

ment would have to depend on physicians' inability to charge different prices for interesting and dull cases.[22]

An important aspect of physician behavior that has been neglected until recently is the ability of the physician to influence the patient's demand for medical care, the agency relationship. If this relationship is perfect (the physician advises consumers solely according to what is the patient's interest), then the observed demand reflects consumer preferences in the usual way. If the physician instead overprescribes services, demand has been artificially increased. If physicians had no scruples or "honesty preference," one would imagine that they would increase the patient's demand as much as possible subject to patient disbelief. If demand is always shifted by the maximum, then the effect of insurance or other variables on utilization is qualitatively similar to the case of the perfect agency relationship. While the levels of utilization before and after an increase in insurance are higher in the former case, demand rises in either case.[23]

A more subtle and useful model assumes that the physician values both income and "honesty."[24] In other words, the physician prefers to act as a perfect agent, but trades off the unpleasantness of giving misleading advice with the added income from doing so. If so, the extent of artificial demand shifting is not constant. However, despite the more complicated agency relationship, the important qualitative aspects of the effects of insurance on utilization remain unchanged.

A model of physician behavior that differs more substantially from the others is the target income or "satisficing" model.[25] In its simplest form, it states that prices and output are set to achieve a target income, somehow predetermined. If demand should change but costs remain the same, price and quantity (and the other dimensions of output) will be unchanged. However, if costs are increased, then price and/or quantity will be adjusted to maintain the target income. While this view might be useful to explain short-run adjustments (or lack of them), it is not very useful in the long run as the target income cannot

---

[22] The empirical findings of Held and Reinhardt, "Health Manpower Policy," tend to diminish the empirical importance of this model. Feldstein's evidence for this phenomenon, inability to estimate a downward-sloping demand function for physician services, has been criticized. Newhouse and Phelps *On Having Your Cake*, appendix D, point out that the demand function is underidentified.

[23] Evans, "Supplier-Induced Demand," discusses the difficulties of comparative static analysis when physicians can shift demand and concludes that little can be said. He does not consider the possibility that demand is always shifted by the maximum amount.

[24] Pauly, "The Role of Demand Creation."

[25] Joseph P. Newhouse, "A Model of Physician Pricing," *Southern Economic Journal*, vol. 37 (October 1970), pp. 174–183.

be considered a given. The target must be less than the maximum, but there appears to be no rule to determine it. If the target is greater than the maximum, then physicians will pursue income maximization.

Assumptions Used in This Study. The assumptions made here on consumer and provider behavior are very simple and straightforward. Basically, we assume that consumers demand more medical care at lower prices, or that the demand curve for medical care slopes downward. We thus ignore the problem of demand creation by physicians through altering the advice given to consumers.

For the providers of medical care, we assume that their behavior can be summarized by profit maximization and costs that rise with output. In the short run (a time period so short that the number of physicians cannot change), physicians may work fewer hours if their incomes rise. We assume that this effect does not occur, consistent with our focus on fundamental long-run features of the supply and demand for medical care after all adjustments have been made. In the case of physicians, an increase in income may lead to less output, but in the long run the entry of new physicians will eventually lead to greater output. Actually, our conclusions would be unaffected by performing the analysis in a short-run framework where output may decrease, except that more complete insurance would lead to higher prices and lower output, rather than higher output.

Our analysis applies both to physicians and to health care institutions or firms such as hospitals. Some may object that hospitals are nonprofit firms and thus cannot be modeled as maximizing profit. This argument is one-half correct: most hospitals are nonprofit firms. However, most theories of nonprofit behavior give analytical results similar to profit maximization for the response of the industry to such changes as increased demand or higher costs.[26] That means that for the prediction of the main response of the hospital industry to national health insurance, treating them as if they were maximizing profits is appropriate.[27]

---

[26] For more on the similar responses in nonprofit and profit-seeking models, see Pauly, "The Behavior of Nonprofit Hospital Monopolies."

[27] H. E. Frech III, "The Case of the Medical Care Industry," in Thomas G. Moore, ed., *Regulatory Reform* (Washington, D.C.: American Enterprise Institute, forthcoming).

APPENDIX B
Graphical Analysis of Some Key Results

Several of the points made in this monograph can be better understood through the aid of a simple graphical analysis. We first examine the initial situation of no insurance, then coinsured service benefits, and finally, indemnity insurance, all with the aid of a basic graphical market analysis.

No Insurance. The initial no-insurance situation leads to an equilibrium price and quantity determined by the interaction of the marginal cost and demand curves, as shown in figure 1. DD is the no-insurance demand curve, DMR the marginal revenue curve, MCMC is the marginal cost curve and P_n, Q_n represent the no-insurance price and quantity.

Coinsured Service Benefits. Coinsured service benefits will cause the demand curve relevant to providers to rotate around its intersection with the quantity axis. Thus, the new demand curve will be DcD, in figure 2. This new demand curve is higher than the original in the following way. At each quantity the consumer is willing to pay the amount given by the height of the no-insurance demand curve. The insurer pays some proportions of the consumer's out-of-pocket expense.[1] Adding the original demand price and the insurance payment gives the new coinsurance demand curve. The insurance payment is a constant proportion of the demand price itself. The fact that the demand curve is higher as a result of the insurance reflects the moral hazard.

The equilibrium quantity is given by Q_c in figure 2, at the intersection of the new marginal revenue curve, MRc, and the marginal cost

---

[1] The proportion paid by the insurer, s, is related to the coinsurance proportion, c, by $s = (1-c)/c$.

FIGURE 1

Price and Quantity of Medical Care: No Insurance

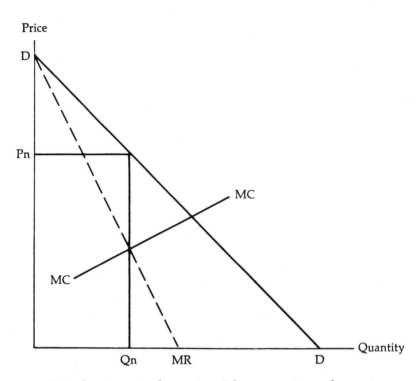

curve. Pc is the corresponding price. Of course, price and quantity are higher than under the no-insurance situation.

Service Mix under Coinsured Service Benefits. The monopoly power of the providers leads to a distortion of service mix in favor of the services that are more elastically demanded. Coinsurance adds to the distortion because it leads to a larger increase in quantity supplied of the more elastically demanded services. This proposition is illustrated in figure 3. Comparing panel (a) with panel (b), both of which represent the same coinsurance rate, it is clear that the larger relative increase in quantity comes from the service which is more elastically demanded.

Indemnity Insurance. The implacement of indemnity insurance causes a parallel upward shift in the demand curve, equal in amount to the amount of the indemnity payment limit. This is displayed in figure 4, where DiDi is the demand curve under indemnity insurance. The

FIGURE 2

Price and Quantity of Medical Care: Coinsured Service Benefits

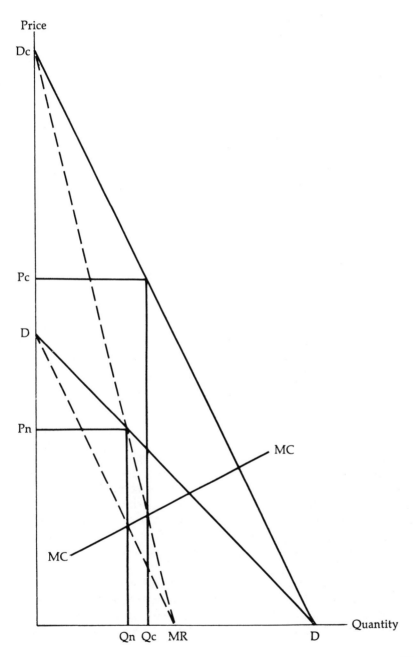

FIGURE 3

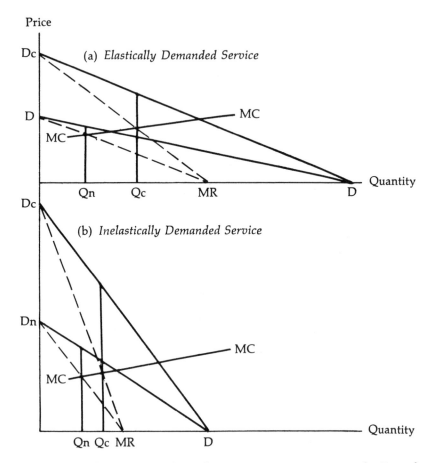

new price and quantity under indemnity insurance are given by Pi and Qi, respectively. As one can see, indemnity insurance raises price and quantity of medical care, just as coinsured service benefits do. However, for the same quantity indemnity insurance raises price *less* than service benefits. To see this, we need a slightly more complicated graphical analysis, which shows both indemnity and service benefits on the same graph, figure 5.

In figure 5, indemnity and service benefit plans which lead to identical quantity, $Q_c = Q_i$, and also to identical out-of-pocket payments for consumers (the shaded area) are compared. As one can easily see, the service benefit plan leads to a much higher price of services.

FIGURE 4

PRICE AND QUANTITY OF MEDICAL CARE: INDEMNITY INSURANCE

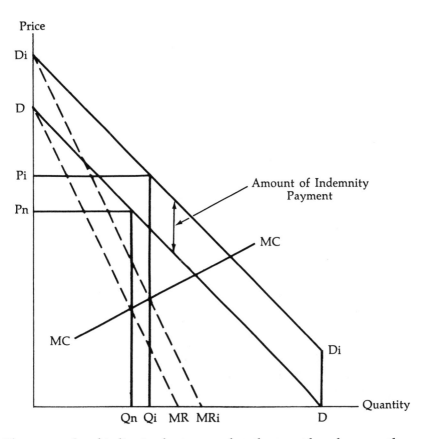

The reason for this lies in the impact that the two plans have on the slope of the demand curves. The service benefit plan makes the demand curve steeper, making it more attractive for suppliers to reduce output and raise prices. Indemnity benefits, on the other hand, do not alter the slope of the demand curve so that there is less incentive for monopolist suppliers to cut back output. This difference between the two plans depends on the assumption that suppliers have some monopoly power. If they did not, then the slope of the demand curves would be irrelevant and the two plans would lead to identical results in this simple analysis.

FIGURE 5

PRICE AND QUANTITY OF MEDICAL CARE: SERVICE BENEFITS VERSUS INDEMNITY INSURANCE

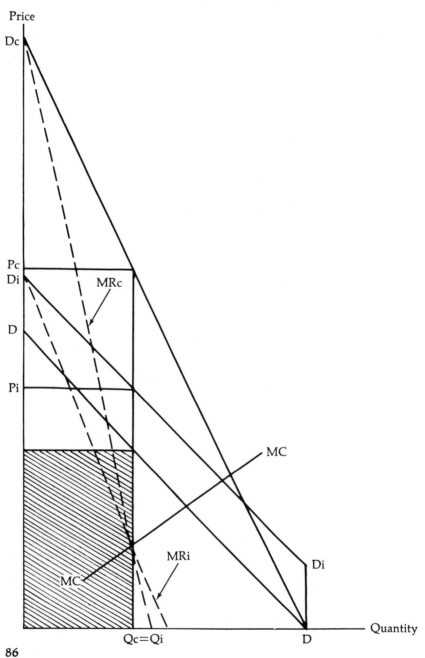

86

APPENDIX C

Mathematical Derivation of Some Key Results for Alternative Types of Health Insurance

Coinsured Service Benefits. One can analyze the impact of coinsured service benefits as a proportional ad valorem subsidy, s, defined as the ratio of the insurance payment to the out-of-pocket payment, $(0 < s < \infty)$. Thus, the coinsurance demand equation becomes

$$p = (1 + s)p(x), \tag{1}$$

where p is the price received by the producer, and x is output.[1] For a representative monopolist, profit is given by

$$\pi = (1 + s)xp(x) - c(x), \tag{2}$$

where $c(x)$ is the cost function, $p_x(x) < 0$, and $c_x(x) > 0$. The first and second order conditions for profit maximization are

$$\frac{d\pi}{dx} = (1 + s)[xp_x(x) + p(x)] - c_x(x) = 0 \tag{3}$$

and

$$\frac{d^2\pi}{dx^2} = (1 + s)[xp_{xx}(x) + 2p_x(x)] - c_{xx}(x) < 0 . \tag{4}$$

To evaluate the effect of coinsured service benefits on output, (3) is totally differentiated with respect to x, obtaining

$$\frac{dx}{ds} = \frac{-[xp_x(x) + p(x)]}{(1 + s)[xp_{xx}(x) + 2p_x(x)] - c_{xx}(x)} . \tag{5}$$

---

[1] In our notation, one would write the conventional coinsurance (proportion of the bill paid by the consumer) as $1/(1 + s)$.

When it is noted that the bracketed term in the numerator is marginal revenue and that the denominator is negative from the second order condition of equation (4), it is clear that dx/ds is always nonnegative. To determine the effects of service benefits on price,[2] we differentiate the demand function (1) with respect to s to obtain

$$\frac{dp}{ds} = p(x) + (1 + s)p_x(x)\frac{dx}{ds} ,\qquad (6)$$

the sign of which is positive by our assumption that $c_{xx}(x) \geq 0$,[3] or that marginal costs do not fall with output. When $c_{xx}(x) < 0$, dp/ds cannot be signed.

It can be shown that service benefits distort the mix of medical services produced. Consider n services that have independent demands $p_j = p_j(x_j)$ and that are produced separately with cost functions $c_j(x_j)$. To avoid complex subscript notation, derivatives are denoted by primes here. Profit maximization is obtained by:

$$\pi = \sum_{j=1}^{n} (1 + s)x_j p_j(x_j) - c_j(x_j) \qquad (7)$$

$$\frac{\partial \pi}{\partial x_j} = (1 + s)[x_j p_j'(x_j) + p_j(x_j)] - c_j'(x_j) = 0 \qquad j = 1, \ldots n \quad (8)$$

$$x_j = \frac{c_j'(x_j) - (1 + s)p_j(x_j)}{(1 + s)p_j'(x_j)} . \qquad (9)$$

---

[2] It should be noted that if providers were permitted to give cash rebates to patients, the tendency for explosive price increases seen for full-coverage service benefits would occur for coinsured service benefits as well.

[3] To sign dp/ds, we substitute for dx/ds in (6). Rearranging terms, and reducing notation by substituting MR, dMR/dx, and dMC/dx when appropriate, the expression

$$\frac{dp}{ds} = \frac{p(x)\left[(1 + s)\dfrac{dMR}{dx} - \dfrac{dMC}{dx}\right] - (1 + s)p_x(x)MR}{(1 + s)\dfrac{dMR}{dx} - \dfrac{dMC}{dx}}$$

is obtained. Setting the above expression >0, multiplying by the (negative) denominator, and rearranging terms leads to:

$$(1 + s)\frac{dMR}{dx} - \frac{dMC}{dx} < \frac{(1 + s)p_x(x)MR}{p(x)} .$$

Solving for dMC/dx, we get:

$$\frac{dMC}{dx} > (1 + s)\left(\frac{dMR}{dx} - \frac{p_x(x)MR}{p(x)}\right).$$

The expression on the right must be negative because the slope of the marginal revenue, dMR/dx, must be more negative than the slope of the demand curve, $p_x(x)$, and also because $1 > dMR/p(x) > 0$. Thus, $c_{xx}(x) \geq 0$ is sufficient but not necessary for $dp/ds > 0$.

Taking any two services, $a \neq b$, output mix is

$$\frac{x_a}{x_b} = \frac{[c_a'(x_a) - (1 + s)p_a(x_a)]p_b'(x_b)}{[c_b'(x_b) - (1 + s)p_b(x_b)]p_a'(x_a)} , \qquad (10)$$

which is a function of s.

Indemnity Insurance Benefits. With indemnity insurance, the demand function, including the per unit insurance subsidy i, becomes

$$p = i + p(x) . \qquad (11)$$

For the profit-maximizing monopolist

$$\pi = xp(x) + ix - c(x) . \qquad (12)$$

To optimize:

$$\frac{d\pi}{dx} = xp_x(x) + p(x) + i - c_x(x) = 0 \qquad (13)$$

$$\frac{d^2\pi}{dx^2} = xp_{xx}(x) + 2p_x(x) - c_{xx}(x) < 0 . \qquad (14)$$

To assess the effect of the indemnity payment on output,

$$\frac{dx}{di} = \frac{-1}{xp_{xx}(x) + 2p_x(x) - c_{xx}(x)} . \qquad (15)$$

From the second-order condition, equation (14), the expression is clearly nonnegative. To assess the effects of indemnity benefits on price, the demand function (11) is differentiated with respect to i and the following is obtained:

$$\frac{dp}{di} = 1 + p_x(x) \frac{dx}{di} . \qquad (16)$$

Using the procedure discussed in footnote 3, the expression can be shown to be nonnegative. As in the case of service benefits, results are similar for pure competition.

An important question is what the relative effects of service and indemnity benefits are on the price of medical care. To assess this, benefit levels (s and i) are set so that the two types of plans lead to the same output. At this output level, the resulting total prices are compared. Since output is the same and costs do not vary with type of insurance, and output is determined where marginal revenue equals marginal cost, marginal revenue is the same for either case. Equating (3) and (13) and collecting terms yields

$$s[xp_x(x) + p(x)] = i .$$ (17)

Referring to the demand functions facing the producer,

$$p = (1 + s)p(x)$$ (1)

and

$$p = i + p(x) ,$$ (11)

the type of insurance benefit that leads to higher market prices, holding quantity constant, will depend upon whether $sp(x)$ or i is larger. From (17), it is clear that this depends upon the sign of $sxp_x(x)$, which is always negative. Consequently, prices are lower under indemnity benefits than under coinsured service benefits at any given output.

Turning to the analysis of product or service mix, the quantity produced of service j under indemnity benefit i is

$$x_j = \frac{c_j'(x_j) - p_j(x_j) - i_j}{p_j'(x_j)} .$$ (18)

The ratio of the quantities of any two services, a and b is

$$\frac{x_a}{x_b} = \frac{[c_a'(x_a) - p_a(x_a) - i_a]p_b'(x_b)}{[c_b'(x_b) - p_b(x_b) - i_b]p_a'(x_a)} .$$ (19)

This shows how varying the indemnity payments for the two services can change output mix. From (19), we can derive a formula for a set of indemnity payments that do not distort output mix. Defining the numerator and denominator of (19) (with i set equal to zero) as D_a and D_b respectively, nondistorting indemnity benefits would require that the indemnity term not change the ratio of quantities:

$$\frac{D_a}{D_b} = \frac{D_a - i_a p_b'(x_b)}{D_b - i_b p_a'(x_a)} ,$$ (20)

which reduces to the following rule:

$$\frac{i_a}{i_b} = \frac{D_a p_a'(x_a)}{D_b p_b'(x_b)} .$$ (21)

From this expression, it is clear that a cost-based relative value scale for indemnity benefits would not avoid distortion of output mix. Of course, in the presence of monopoly, the right distortion could actually improve matters.

Regulation of Medical Prices: Fee Schedules. Consider the case where consumers are fully covered for medical care expenditures and where producers are effectively barred from demanding extra payments or varying the quality level of service. Then, monopolist producers will produce the quantity of services where

$$p^* = c_x(x) \ . \tag{22}$$

An increase in the regulated price will increase output (up to the level consumers are willing to accept for free).

If a separate charge can be levied on patients, the producer's profit function becomes

$$\pi = [\hat{p}(x) + p^*]x - c(x) \ , \tag{23}$$

where $\hat{p}$ reflects the direct charge to the consumer, p^* is the regulated price paid by the insurer, and $(\hat{p} + p^*)$ is the total price received. However, (23) is exactly the same function as (12)—indemnity benefits without price regulation. In the present case, p^* corresponds to the indemnity payment, i. Thus we can assert that when cash transfers are permitted, a system of service benefits with regulated prices (payment by the insurer) is equivalent to indemnity benefits.

If separate charges above the regulated rate are not allowed, producers can, in reality, alter the attractiveness and quality of the care provided. In order to model this case, assume that amenities or quality cannot be separately priced. The provider faces a demand function

$$x = x(y) \tag{24}$$

and a cost function

$$c = c(x,y) \ , \tag{25}$$

where y reflects the quality attributes of output. Assume that

$$x_y, c_x, c_y > 0, x_{yy} \leq 0, c_{xx}, c_{yy}, \text{ and } c_{xy} \geq 0 \ .$$

Since price is fixed, the producer chooses either quantity or quality through optimizing calculations, and then obtains the other through the demand equation. Profits are

$$\pi = p^*x - c(x,y) . \tag{26}$$

Maximizing profits with respect to quality yields

$$\frac{d\pi}{dy} = p^*x_y - c_x x_y - c_y = 0 . \tag{27}$$

This condition states that the marginal revenue from the last unit of quality change (through increasing quantity sold) must equal the marginal cost of additional quality (including the cost of the additional units produced). The second-order condition is

$$\frac{d^2\pi}{dy^2} = x_{yy}(p^* - c_x) - [x_y^2 c_{xx} + 2x_y c_{xy} + c_{yy}] < 0 . \tag{28}$$

To assess the effect of a change in the regulated price (or the effect of regulation) on quality, (27) is totally differentiated with respect to price. After rearranging terms, we obtain

$$\frac{dy}{dp^*} = \frac{-x_y}{A} , \tag{29}$$

where A is the second-order condition and $A < 0$. This is clearly positive. Thus, an increase in the regulated price will increase quality as producers find it more profitable to attract patients and increase quality to do so. Since $x_y > 0$, the quantity of services will also increase with a rise in the regulated price.[4]

"Usual, Customary, and Prevailing" Price Regulation: An Attempt to Create a Dynamic, Market-Based Price System. The "usual, customary, and prevailing" (UCP) price regulation system contains analytically predictable dynamic mechanisms.

Assume that suppliers can charge patients more than the indemnity level 1 and act independently, so that they ignore the effect of

---

[4] These unambiguous results of the regulated price under imposed insurance do not carry over to the usual case of regulation without subsidy. Simply adding p^* to the demand function in the above model leads to ambiguous results for both dy/dp^* and dx/dp^*, the signs of which depend on the cross partial derivative, x_{p^*y}. See White, "Quality Variation When Prices Are Regulated."

their prices on future insurance levels. This assumption is reasonable and necessary if the mechanism is to produce fees which vary over time. The simplest way to treat the UCP method is to assume that all providers set identical fees so that the insurer need only observe total market price in one period and use that price as the indemnity insurance payment in the next period. In period t_0, the market price will be given by

$$P_{t_0} = i + p(x) . \tag{11}$$

Note that as long as consumers are consuming less medical care than the saturation amount, $(p(x) > 0)$, $P_{t_0} > i$. Using the UCP system, the insurer sets the price for period t_1 at the previously prevailing market price, P_{t_0}, so that the market price in the next period becomes

$$P_{t_1} = P_{t_0} + p(x) . \tag{30}$$

Again, if $p(x) > 0, P_{t_1} > P_{t_0}$. Thus the market price keeps rising under a UCP system until, as x increases, equilibrium is reached where $p(x) = 0$, the point where the marginal value of medical care to consumers is zero. (If the demand function does not include such a point at finite quantity, prices will continue to rise without limit.)

The speed of these rate increases will depend upon the percentile chosen and the frequency of revision of prevailing rates.